CYBERCULTURE

PROTECT YOURSELF FROM TROLLS, SHAMERS, BULLIES AND STALKERS

C.D.BELL & S.L.BELL

PINK PARROT PUBLISHING

TASMANIA

© 2018

PUBLISHED BY PINK PARROT PUBLISHING

PINKPARROTPUBLISHING.COM

PINKPARROT@PINKPARROTPUBLISHING.COM

TASMANIA, AUSTRALIA

THIS MATERIAL IS ADAPTED FROM COURSEWORK FOR MEDIA ENTREPRENEURS

PRINT ISBN: 978-0-9873128-5-3

Contents

Hate is everywhere on the internet and it's getting worse.

Cybergangs trawl the web for victims to destroy; online lynch mobs get people fired from their jobs; school kids are bullied to death; hackers reconfigure web pages to give epileptics seizures, and RIP trolls viciously deface Facebook memorial pages set up to honour dead teenagers.

How has it come to this?

The internet was never meant to be a playground for bullies, thugs, and psychopaths. In fact, its original purpose was to exchange raw data between researchers. Over the years, it evolved to allow information sharing among the masses, but its democratic ethos also invited the darker side of human nature to the online table, with devastating consequences.

It's so bad now that any one of us can become the target of an online tormentor, bully, or stalker. And it's not as if we have to do anything dire to incur the internet's wrath. Some have simply posted ill-conceived jokes that the cybermob deliberately misinterpreted and others have given well-intentioned opinions for which they were vilified mercilessly.

So what, if anything, can we do to protect ourselves from trolls, bullies, cybermobs and stalkers before cyberspace becomes a no-go zone?

Cyberculture answers these questions and more and offers practical and innovative suggestions to help us stay safe online. It delves into the crucial differences between the different types of internet menace and why they each must be managed differently.

Via case studies and recent research, Cyberculture reveals the shocking effect trolling, cybershaming, and cyberstalking has on its victims and perpetrators as well as what law enforcement and governments are doing—and not doing—to curb the hostility.

Whether you're online for business, education, or pleasure, Cyberculture will give you the knowledge and skills to navigate, and possibly help redeem, an increasingly hostile and unforgiving internet.

TROLLS

Welcome to the online world of trolls, bullies, shamers and stalkers, all of whom can be dangerous to your mental and physical health.

First up, we will examine trolls and the effect they have on their targets. This will inlclude:

- The features of troll psychology and behaviour
- The difference between trolls, cyberbullies and cyberstalkers
- The types of trolls
- What motivates individuals to troll
- Online self-defence strategies to counter trolls

Online trolls come in several varieties, some familiar and others surprising, and we'll look at who they target, what they say, when they say it, and why they say it.

While trolls can be crude, nasty, and provocative--although some can be genuinely funny--they are nowhere near as malevolent and sinister as their online cousin, the cyberstalker, who we'll meet later, along with the cyberbully, another kind of online tormentor.

Finally, we'll examine trolling's effect on its victims and on the trolls themselves and discuss useful self-defence strategies.

TROLL TIMELINE

1983-1990

The Internet is young, troll-free and populated by scientists, computer geeks and academics who either know each other or know each other's connections.

AUGUST 6, 1991

Internet opens to the public.

DECEMBER 14, 1992

First verifiable use of the word "trolling" in an internet context appears with someone from early discussion board Usenet's urban legend forum alt.folklore.urban writing: "Maybe after I post it, we could go trolling some more and see what happens."

This likely refers to the game of "trolling for newbies", where the group's older members would ask inane questions to bait newcomers

2003-2006

Social media sites and blogs proliferate and trolls begin to infiltrate discussion threads and people's personal accounts.

2007-2017

Troll activity increases at a furious pace. Celebrities begin to leave social media due to the constant harassment and intimidation. Comment sections on blogs and news-sites are shut down and we begin to wonder if the trolls have finally won

Professor Mary Beard and the extreme end of trolling

Mary Beard is a highly respected classics professor at Cambridge University. She's authored many books, including *Pompeii* and *Meet The Romans*, and written and presented several popular history documentaries for the BBC. At 62, her hair is long and grey and her face Botox-free. She wears no makeup and says she is happy to look her age.

In 2013, she appeared on the BBC1 panel show *Question Time* where she challenged reports that immigrants were straining public services in the Lincolnshire town of Boston. Soon after, she became the recipient of what *Daily Mail* journalist Jane Fryer called "…one of the most truly monstrous episodes of internet trolling ever" on social media.

Comments on the *Don't Start Me Off* website, for example, named her "Twat of the Week" and included shocking personal insults about her body, sexual orientation and family. She was called "a vile, spiteful excuse for a woman, who eats too much cabbage and has cheese straws for teeth," and "a disgrace to Cambridge University and woman-kind."

It also published pictures of hairy legs and female genitalia over which was superimposed an image of her head.

"There were more "c" words and "f" words and "p" words than you can imagine."~ Professor Mary Beard

Someone also threatened to blow up her house and gave her the exact time and date. She took the threat seriously and evacuated her family at the appointed time.

Beard was gobsmacked by all the hate and decided to fight back and "stand up for myself and other women." On her blog *A Don's Life*, she suggested that people inundate Don't Start Me Off with comments or Latin poetry, which they did in droves. This led its co-founder and moderator, businessman Richard White, to accuse Beard's supporters of being trolls themselves. Soon after, the website closed

Despite her strong stand against the trolls, however, she prefers to shame rather than prosecute them and for all of us to adopt a more civilised online discourse.

Beard's pro-active stance is one example of how people fight back against trolls.

TROLL ETYMOLOGY

In Old French of the 1500s, "troller" was a hunting term and meant to "wander, to go in quest of game without purpose." From the 1560s, it gained fishing connotations, with the sense of "to lure on as with a moving bait, entice, allure."

The first recorded use of the word "troll" in modern English is from a court document (c 1600s) where Catherine, a woman from the Shetlands, was accused of "airt and pairt of witchcraft and sorcerie, in hanting and seeing the Trollis ryse out of the kyrk yeard of Hildiswick."

THE MODERN TROLL

Troll-like behaviour has always existed, whether it's slapping graffiti on toilet doors or public buildings, making prank phone calls, acting the class clown, or knocking on people's doors and running away.
It's the digital equivalent of the ancient trickster figure whose behaviour can range from the amusing to the hateful.

Today, "to troll" in an internet context still retains its original sense of baiting, although the bait these days is laid for people rather than for fish or game.

TROLLS, CYBERBULLIES AND CYBERSTALKERS: YES, THERE IS A DIFFERENCE

A crucial distinction must be made between online trolls, cyberbullies and cyberstalkers. While they each appear similar to their victims and elicit similar emotional responses from them, they behave differently and have different psychological needs.

TROLLS

Trolls visit blogs, forums, social media platforms, chatrooms and websites in order to confuse, send-up, disrupt, divert, or inflame conversations with off-topic, sarcastic, critical, sexist, racist, or outrageous comments, all for the fun of eliciting a response.

Generally speaking, trolls and their victims do not know each other. Trolls want the spotlight on them and are indifferent to the harm or

INTERNET TROLL
A mythological internet being
that lives under an internet
bridge. Loves to hunt for innocent
netizens. Common tactics:
antagonizing other netizens by
posting racist or offensive
comments.
The Urban Dictionary

confusion their comments cause. They don't care who they upset as long as they upset someone. As Professor Mary Beard observed, *"It was such generic, violent misogyny. In a way, I didn't feel it was about me."*

Trolls range from the funny to the hateful and, like the mythical Trickster, like to play pranks, disrupt online communities and typically harass, deceive and provoke people for their own amusement

Trolls want a reaction from their target, will usually leave one-off comments and will troll elsewhere if the person or online community fails to rise to the bait, at least on that specific occasion.

If they persist in harassing a particular individual or group for any length of time, however, they cease to be trolls and become cyberbullies or cyberstalkers instead.

Usually, the maxim *"Don't take the bait. Don't feed the trolls"* works with these people because they are motivated by the pleasure derived from their target's angry or hurt response. If denied this pleasure, they will move on and try to provoke someone else, at least on that occasion.

CYBERBULLIES

Although bullying can happen to anyone at any age, cyberbullying generally refers to children or teenagers who bully other children or teenagers.

Cyberbullies usually know their victim and try to get under their skin by calling them hateful names or posting vicious rumors about them.

Cyberbullies might also publish embarrassing pictures of their target on social media or threaten to physically hurt them. Cyberbullies drive some of their victims to suicide.

We will look at cyberbullies and their tactics in a future chapter.

CYBERSTALKERS

Cyberstalkers are the internet's most dangerous and persistent predator. These individuals have an emotional fixation on a specific person from whom they demand a response. Like Terminators, they will not stop until their target is damaged emotionally, physically, or professionally. They can be lone wolves with a vendetta or part of a world-wide stalker syndicate where they compete with each other to see who can upset their target the most.

Members of stalker syndicates see themselves as a kind of online mafia and their primary motivation is entertainment.

Lone cyberstalkers, on the other hand, are more likely to be motivated by rage, revenge, money, envy, or jealousy.

Cyberstalkers, like cyberbullies, may upload private videos featuring their victim, post hateful messages, or spread malicious rumours. They might send videos and photos to their target privately and then, for maximum dramatic impact, threaten public exposure. They may post their victim's address and social security number online (called "doxing"), threaten to murder their family and, in an act that is bound to kill someone eventually, call emergency services to their home. This is known as "swatting".

Cyberstalkers may or may not know their victim personally.

Cyberstalkers not only want to hurt, humiliate and upset their target they want to outright destroy them. They want negative attention focused exclusively on their victim rather than on themselves.

The maxim, "Don't take the bait. Don't feed the trolls" rarely works with cyberstalkers because they are not trolls. In fact, it often makes the situation worse because they are so invested in gaining the attention of a particular person that their behaviour escalates if they are blocked, muted, or ignored by their target.

We will look at cyberstalkers and how to deal with them in more detail in Chapter 4.

WHERE DO WE FIND TROLLS?
Trolls are everywhere online in chatrooms and forum discussions, comment threads on blogs, news sites, and YouTube videos, dating sites, and on all forms of social media including Facebook, Instagram, Reddit, and Twitter.

Who are they, really?

Although many trolls conform to the young, disaffected white male stereotype, a surprising number turn out to be what journalist Jon Ronson calls "nice people like us"

According to Whitney Phillips, Professor of Literature at Mercer University:

"Trolls are portrayed as aberrational and antithetical to how normal people converse with each other. And that could not be further from the truth. These mostly normal people do things that seem fun at the time that have huge implications. You want to say this is the bad guys, but it's a problem of us."

THE TROLL STEREOTYPE: WHITE, MALE, UNEMPLOYED, AND ISOLATED

In 2014, John Nimmo, a 25-year-old unemployed recluse, was sentenced to eight weeks' jail for sending threatening tweets to Caroline Criado-Perez, a prominent feminist who had supported a campaign to feature a woman on British bank notes.

His tweets included: *"Shut up bitch"* and *"Ya not that gd looking to rape u be fine."*

His lawyer, Paul Kennedy, described his client as a man of hitherto good character who was: *"...a social recluse, that is exactly what he is really. He rarely leaves the house but to empty the bins. He sits in the house 24/7, he has nothing to do, he claims benefits, he is a somewhat sad individual."*

NOT YOUR STEREOTYPICAL TROLL

Brenda Leyland was a smart, educated woman who went to church, loved to garden, and was active in her village community. A divorcee with two grown sons, she had attended a Catholic convent school and London University.

In a period of four years, however, she used the Twitter ID @sweepyface to send or resend hundreds of tweets about Gerry and Kate McCann whose daughter Madeline (3) disappeared while they were on holiday in Portugal in 2007. Some days she posted as many as 50 tweets, many of which implied that the McCanns were involved in their daughter's disappearance. After a reporter from Skynews exposed her @sweepyface identity, she committed suicide in a local hotel in October 2014.

Although her social class, level of community involvement and education do not fit the accepted troll profile, she did possibly exhibit the troll characteristic of loneliness, with one neighbour describing her as "lonely beyond belief".

"When Madeleine first went missing she used to go over to her home village all the time. She used to go to the local pub and the shops telling everyone what she thought about the family. It seemed very odd behaviour." Brenda Leyland's neighbour.

Brenda Leyland's story suggests that our idea of the stereotypical troll is limited and, if an educated, middle-class woman could behave like this, is it possible we could all troll given the right circumstances?

The Bored Troll

Isabella Sorley was a 23-year-old university graduate when convicted of sending menacing tweets to a high profile feminist. In 2014, she was sentenced to 12 weeks jail.

When asked why she did it, she said she was " *off her face" drunk"* and *"bored"* when she tweeted: *""f*** off and die you worthless piece of crap", "go kill yourself"* and *"rape is the last of your worries".*

The Funny Troll

Tech website Gizmodo calls Ken M *"the most epic troll on the internet."* In real life, he's Kenneth McCarthy, a 37-year-old copywriter for *Comedy Central.*

Since 2011, Ken M's deposited deliberately tongue-in-cheek, clueless comments over vast swathes of the social media landscape. He has a huge following and a reputation as *"the world's least informed commentator."*

He is neither rude, abusive nor bellicose and his Ken M. character suggests an "ornery, befuddled grandfather",-- an impression reinforced by his innocuous display picture--rather than a nasty troll.

McCarthy says he never even knew what a troll was when he began leaving comments on Yahoo as a way to counter what he calls *"it's toxic, shitty space."*

He still enjoys trolling Yahoo spaces and the *"humorless and pedantic"* Huffington Post commenters, because he wants to make people laugh and to take themselves less seriously.

Grammar Trolls

Grammar trolls correct other people's grammar, spelling, punctuation, and word choice errors. They tend to be indifferent to the actual topic under discussion and instead home in on errant apostrophes, dangling participles, or misplaced commas. Some of these trolls are aggressive and obnoxious and derive pleasure from their target's humiliation. Others are well-meaning and harmless. At their best, grammar trolls unintentionally provide their victims with free proofreading advice.

WHEN ARE PEOPLE MOST LIKELY TO TROLL?

Recent research from Stanford University suggests that anyone can troll given the presence of certain factors.

Researchers analysed thousands of CNN comments and surveyed 667 participants to see when people are most likely to troll.

They discovered three main elements that incite troll behaviour:

- **Mood:** We're more likely to troll when we feel bad. And the worse we feel, the worse we troll. What's more, if we've been involved in discussions that feature troll comments, we are more likely to go on to make negative remarks elsewhere online.
- **Time of day:** Troll activity peaks on Mondays and is more common late at night and these times coincide with when we're more likely to be in a bad mood.
- **Tone of initial comments:** When threads begin with an abusive comment, they are twice as likely to be trolled by other participants later on compared to a discussion that starts with a neutral or positive comment

Researchers also found that if people were in a bad mood while they viewed negative posts, they were significantly more likely to troll either on that comment thread or another thread elsewhere.

Researchers concluded that mood and discussion context taken together are a better predictor of troll behaviour than a person's trolling history.

Troll Victim - Zelda Williams

On August 11, 2014, the actor Robin Williams hanged himself with a belt in his California home. For several years prior to his suicide, he'd suffered from Lewy body demential. A devastating and debilitating brain disease with no cure and no effective treatment.

Shortly after his death, his daugher Zelda deleted her Twitter and Instagram accounts.She had received abusive comments and fake picture of a dead body in a morgue. They had been photoshopped to look like Robin Williams.

"Somewhere along the way to the web's starry-eyed promise of a connected world, we lost track of common decency." ~ Erin Griffith, Journalist

WHY DO PEOPLE TROLL?

10 REASONS WHY

1. The Dark Tetrad

Some people are simply more difficult than others and more likely to post confronting online comments.

A 2014 research paper from the University of Manitoba found correlations between the Dark Tetrad personality traits of Machiavellianism (a propensity to deceive and manipulate others), psychopathy (a lack of guilt or remorse), narcissism (vainglory and entitlement), and sadism (pleasure in the suffering of others) with sadism being the most common troll characteristic.

The researchers concluded: "Sadists just want to have fun...and the internet is their playground."

It's worth noting, however, that only 5.6 percent of participants actually specified that they enjoyed trolling, with 41.3 percent of users happy to be "non-commenters", suggesting that hardcore, sadistic trolls are in the minority.

2. The online disinhibition effect

John Suler, professor of psychology at Rider University, identifies six reasons why we become more uninhibited online:

- **"You don't know me"** The online world is relatively anonymous and makes us feel safe and more willing to experiment with different personas and behaviours. We let down our defences and sometimes act in uncharacteristically strange and surprising ways.
- **"You can't see me"** No one can see or hear us on the Internet unless we want them to. This means people have no access to our body language or voice tone, both of which signal our truthfulness and emotional state. This presents possibilities that do not exist in face-to-face interaction.
- **"See you later"** When it's possible to write dramatic, emotional content and then log out without waiting to see other people's responses, we avoid negative comments and feedback. This allows us to be more candid and explicit online than we are offline because we do not have to deal with other people's reactions.
- **"It's all in my head"** With no voice tone or body language to guide us, we experience people's online written messages as voices in our head—our own familiar voice—and this invites us to relax and be more trusting because the entire Interent sounds like us.
- **"It's just a game"** Some of us play cyberspace as a game where the normal social rules no longer apply. In this make-believe space, we feel more inclined to escape into different characters and to behave in ways we would not allow offline. In other words, we can be anyone we want to be.
- **"Your rules don't apply here"** In the real physical world, we are clear about who is in charge because authority figures walk, talk and dress with authority. In contrast, it's hard to tell who's boss online. What's more, even though we might know someone's offline authority status, we are much less likely to feel intimidated by him or her online. The internet offers a more-or-less equal playing field for everyone and because of this, we see others as peers and open up to them more.

3. Emotional Contagion

Emotional contagion is one of the primary initiators of mob behaviour. If the majority of a group's participants act negatively, it's likely the whole group will act more negatively as well. Some of the most intense and vicious online trolling occurs in the group-think context.

Emotional contagion occurs outside our conscious control and is caused by brain cells called mirror neurons. Mirror neurons fire in exactly the same way whether we watch someone do something or we actually do it ourselves. And it all happens under the cognitive radar unless we're aware of what's going on and take steps to counter it.

So if we spend time in bitter, sarcastic or angry forums, our mirror neurons will have us behave in that way too. And even if we despise what's happening and resist the negativity, it's stressful for the brain to maintain its struggle against such a powerful, primitive biological process.

4. Boredom

"If you had set out to design a way of bringing bored, dissatisfied people up against others flaunting their supposedly more interesting lives, you could hardly have done better than social media – businesses purpose-built for killing time and showing off." ~ Gaby Hinsliff, Journalist

Some of us have too much time on our hands and seek stimulation online where it is quickly and easily acquired. Others find their jobs mundane and look for excitement in cyberspace.

Boredom's ability to turn "nice people like us" into trolls is both insidious and remarkably common.

Several years ago, the University of Limerick ran an experiment where participants were given a boring, repetitive task, after which they were told to suggest punishments for a fictional Englishman convicted of bashing an Irishman. The longer the time participants had spent on the repetitive task, the more likely they were to demand a tough and bloody punishment for the Englishman.

5. Densensitisation

As online hostility worsens, we become numb to all the vitriol and numb to the effect our actions have on others. This means we're more likely to heap on the abuse in a discussion thread because we imagine one more negative comment will make little difference.

6. Anger

Just as some people are more difficult than others, some have a lower anger threshold. Minor annoyances and frustrations trigger these individuals and make them more likely to troll.

The American Psychological Association explains the psychology behind anger:

"People who are easily angered generally have what some psychologists call a low tolerance for frustration, meaning simply that they feel that they should not have to be subjected to frustration, inconvenience, or annoyance. They can't take things in stride, and they're particularly infuriated if the situation seems somehow unjust: for example, being corrected for a minor mistake."

7. Unconscious feelings of inferiority

We're mired in a society where unemployment is high and a university degree no longer guarantees a secure, well-paid job. This, coupled with sky-high property prices that keep home ownership out of reach and a relentless focus on youth, beauty and success leads certain individuals to feel poorly treated and disenfranchised.

This breeds a sense of injustice and can make some people resentful enough to want to hurt or humiliate those who appear more prosperous, happy and successful. Trolls who belittle others because they feel unconsciously inferior like to their victims and make them feel as miserable as they do.

8. Attention-seeking

Trolls crave attention, positive or negative, and the more of it the better. They want the spotlight focused on them and goad their victims to re-post their comments and write blog posts or status updates about them. Even if their target responds positively, the troll usually finds a way to up the ante and the cycle of attention-seeking continues.

9. The Kool-Aid Point

The Kool-Aid Point was coined by the US-based Java Programming instructor and video game developer Kathy Sierra to describe *"a hypothetical threshold point at which the public perception of a popular brand, politician or celebrity becomes unfavourable due to its sheer popularity rather than as a result of valid criticism against it."*

The concept comes from the famous American/English colloquialism "to drink the Kool-Aid", which refers negatively to any person or group who succumbs to peer pressure and follows a perilous or ill-fated idea.

Sierra hypothesised that hardcore trolls emerge at the precise moment they perceive a brand's users or a public figure's followers have "drunk the Kool-Aid" and have fallen hopelessly in love with the product, person or brand.

Sierra believes the Kool-Aid Point is especially risky for successful women: *"I now believe the most dangerous time for a woman with online visibility is the point at which others are seen to be listening, "following", "liking", "favoriting", retweeting. In other words, the point at which her readers have (in the troll's mind) "drunk the Koolaid".*

"From their angry, frustrated point of view, the idea that others listen to you is insanity...You must be stopped. And if they cannot stop you, they can at least ruin your quality of life."

10. Social rewards
Research by Evita March, a lecturer in psychology at Federation University, Australia, focused on the idea of social rewards as a way to explain troll motivation.

Social rewards come in two types: typical and atypical.

Typical social rewards are those we experience when we help others in practical and benevolent ways.

People who look for typical social rewards like to encourage social harmony and civility.

Atypical social rewards--also known as "negative social potency"--are those we experience when we cause social discord through egotistical, self-seeking behaviours.

People who look for atypical social rewards like to inflict emotional pain on others.

March's research team had 396 adults (75.9% women and 24.10% men) complete a questionnaire that measured their level of narcissism, psychopathy, Machiavellianism and sadism.

The team also gauged each participant's desire for atypical social rewards and their propensity for Facebook trolling.

The researchers found, unsurprisingly, that men are more likely than women to troll on Facebook and that trolls are more likely to be sadists and psychopaths.

What did surprise them, however, was that when they included atypical social rewards into their model, they found its effect was far stronger than the effects of psychopathy and sadism as a troll motivator.
Say the researchers:

"This means that while antisocial personality traits do play a role, what really influences trolling behaviour is the social pleasure derived from knowing that others are annoyed by it. The more negative social impact the troll has, the more their behaviour is reinforced."

Evita March's study has important implications for how to combat trolls and we'll explore this in more detail later.

TROLL TACTICS

Linguistics professor and troll expert Claire Hardaker identifies several troll tactics.

Trolls:
- Go off-topic and frustrate everyone with pointless comments, inane observations, or circular argumen
- Use hypocrisy to trigger others. For example, they will criticise someone's spelling, grammar or punctuation while themselves deliberately making the same mistakes to provoke exasperated responses.
- Become the Devil's advocate and uphold a contrary position to the group. This involves deception and manipulation and is likely to cause emotional distress and moral dilemmas.
- Shock others by introducing grossly insensitive, hurtful, or taboo subjects. The comments are so egregious that it often causes the group or individual to retaliate rather than to ignore the provocation even though a response is exactly what the troll wants.
- Cross-post and send identical offensive or provocative messages to multiple groups and wait for the response.
- Give deliberately incorrect advice in answer to people's questions on forums in order to create chaos.

OVERVIEW

As we discussed earlier, trolls leave disruptive, off-topic, abusive and occasionally funny comments on blogs, forums, news sites, social media platforms, chatrooms and websites. They do this for their own amusement and to provoke, confuse or upset their targets. If no-one takes the bait, they find someone else to harass, at least on that occasion.

Trolls prefer to have the spotlight on themselves rather than on their target. Trolls can be mean and hateful, but are less persistent than cyberbullies and far less dangerous than their internet cousin, the cyberstalker.

"Trolls are turning social media and comment boards into a giant locker room in a teen movie, with towel-snapping racial epithets and misogyny." ~ Doc Searls, journalist

Case Study: Arvida Bystrom

Arvida Bystrom is a 26-year-old Swedish model, artist and photographer who posts photos of herself on Instagram that highlight her body hair and cellulite as a way to counter gender stereotypes and constraints.

In 2017, she appeared with unshaven legs in an Adidas Originals ad on YouTube. A barrage of rape and death threats soon followed. She was called "*a monkey*", a "*dirty feminist imbecile*" and told she was "*the most disgusting lady I've ever seen in my whole life.*"

In the video, she describes femininity as a cultural construct and that society is scared of people who challenge this construct. The YouTube comments below the video--some of which include, "h*orrible! Burn it with fire!*", "*shave your legs b*tch*" "*f*** off feminist scum*", "*disgustin*'", "*good luck getting a boyfriend*" and "Swedish anti-rape tactic"-- reinforce her observation. The private messages she received on Instagram were much worse, she said, although this was tempered by lots of supportive messages too.

ARE WOMEN MORE LIKELY TO BE TROLLED THAN MEN?

Not necessarily. Plenty of men are trolled, too, as we'll soon see. But trolls do admit to finding women easier to upset.

Female journalists also appear to cop a huge amount of online hate.

WOMEN IN MEDIA

Female journalists are routinely and aggressively targeted by trolls and cyberstalkers.

A study by Women in Media surveyed nearly 1000 women who work in the Australian media. 41 percent of in-house journalists said they had been harassed, bullied or trolled on social media while 18 percent of freelancers have been cyberstalked.

Some of the journalists described the social media attacks:

"I was sent rape and death threats, had my email hacked."

"I was followed out by a man who took photos of me and my friends – this was after months of being defamed online. I was forced to call the police to intervene."

"Emails with descriptions of the bus my son catches to school, threats of rape."

"It's had a huge impact, including being the cause of changing my career as a journalist."

"Stalkers have arrived at work and said they had an appointment to be interviewed by me. They were escorted off premises by security. Once somebody knocked on my front door and gave my flatmate a 'gift' for me: it was a large bullet from an automatic weapon."

"Man sent more than 400 messages to me on Facebook, asked to move in with me and my partner, worked out where we lived and printed pictures of me and my partner kissing and distributed them."

Case Study: Ginger Gorman

In 2010, Award-winning Australian journalist Ginger Gorman interviewed a gay couple with a 5-year-old son as part of a report on the marginalisation and mistreatment of LGBTI people. Her report aired on ABC radio and was also published online. In 2013, after an investigation by Queensland police and US authorities, the couple were found to be part of an international paedophile ring, convicted and sentenced to jail.

Gorman's original article was still online and found by a conservative US commentator who happened to have thousands of Twitter followers. Gorman began to receive lots of hateful and threatening tweets that called her "incompetent", a "pedophile lover" and enabler and a "dimwit". People wrote hateful blog posts about her and, one night, someone sent her a tweet that said, *"Your life is over."*

Then a picture of her young family appeared on a fascist website.

"At the time, the threat seemed omnipresent. The fear was indescribable."

Gorman eventually sought advice from Alastair MacGibbon who at the time was Director of the Centre for Internet Safety at the University of Canberra. MacGibbon is a former federal police officer with a background in high-tech crime and he is now the Special Adviser to the Prime Minister on Cyber Security.

WHY ARE WOMEN MORE LIKELY TO BE TARGETED?
In 2014, Professor Mary Beard, who we met in Part 1, gave a speech at the British Museum entitled *"Oh, Do Shut Up Dear!"* which looked at the many ways men have sought to silence women since antiquity. Social media, she says, is just the latest avenue through which men attempt to do this.

Beard says it does not matter what women say, it is the simple fact that she is saying anything at all that riles many men.

Her contention is reinforced by a 2016 study conducted by digital security firm Norton. The survey of 1053 women discovered that:

- Nearly half of them had experienced online abuse and harassment in the form of trolling, cyberbullying [sic] and unwanted contact. Over 76 percent were under 30
- They were more likely to be harassed over gender or physical appearance than men
- One in seven had received general threats of physical violence; one in four were under 30
- Women received twice as many death threats and threats of sexual violence than men
- One in four serious and violent threats directed at women related to gender with only 1 in 16 for men.
- 1 in 5 women received attacks on their physical appearance
- 70 percent said online harassment was a serious problem in 2016. 60 percent said it is getting worse
- After being harassed, one in five (22 percent) felt depressed and five percent felt suicidal.

The study's creators said that online harassment of women is at risk of becoming "an established norm in our society." Women under 30 are particularly at risk.

TROLLS VIEW WOMEN AS EASY GAME

Ginger Gorman, the journalist featured in the previous case study, interviewed several professional trolls who work in gangs and spend many hours each week looking for victims to harass online. They target women in particular because they are perceived as more fragile and easier to upset.

"Mark" (not his real name) is a member of a powerful cyberhate gang that targets women because they are:

"…generally weaker [and] more easily offended and easier to anger and stuff like that…generally you can say something about their kids which is gonna set them off pretty quickly. Like you could post what school they go to and stuff like that. That's gonna get them really angry."

People like Mark and his cohorts are more accurately known as cyberstalkers and we'll deal with them in a subsequent chapter.

ARE MORE TROLLS MEN?

Until recently, just about every troll study found that men were more likely to troll than women.

A 2016 online survey of 357 Australian adults who use the dating site Tinder, however, surprised researchers when it found that women and men were equally likely to troll others on the app.
Say the researchers:

" It's unclear at the moment as to why women are engaging in similar amounts of trolling behaviours as men are on Tinder…Perhaps Tinder users are viewed as easy trolling targets, due to the "desperate" stigma that some people still associate with online dating."

MEN GET TROLLED TOO

In another survey, Norton found that more Australian men than women report experiencing online abuse or harassment.
The online survey of around 1,000 Australian men revealed that:

- 54% of respondents had experienced some form of abuse or harassment online
- Among men under 30, the reported incidence was 78%.
- Gay, bisexual, transgender and men from religious minorities were more prone to harassment than other men were with 23 percent attacked over their sexual orientation (only 7 percent of heterosexual

men are).

- Men are less likely to report online harassment than women
- Only 53% of men said online harassment was a serious problem, compared with 70% of women.

HIGH PROFILE MEN ARE PRIME TROLL TARGETS

Research from the think-tank Demos revealed that high-profile men are among the most frequent victims of Twitter abuse.

According to Carl Miller, who conducted the study:

"The fact that male celebrities got more abuse did feel counterintuitive, I think mainly because a lot of the highly publicised cases of trolling and convictions in recent years – Stella Creasy, Caroline Criado-Perez, Mary Beard – have focused specifically on rape threats. That has been a very nasty part of the story of the rise of trolling, but it isn't the full story."

Stephen Fry

Actor and journalist Stephen Fry left Twitter in February 2016 after receiving an onslaught of abuse over a joke he made onstage at an awards ceremony.

On his blog, he said:

"Let us grieve at what Twitter has become. A stalking ground for the sanctimoniously self-righteous who love to second-guess, to leap to conclusions and be offended – worse, to be offended on behalf of others they do not even know. It's as nasty and unwholesome a characteristic as can be imagined. It doesn't matter whether they think they're defending women, men, transgender people, Muslims, humanists … the ghastliness is absolutely the same."

Matt Lucas

British comedian Matt Lucas closed his Twitter account in 2012 after a sixteen-year-old tweeted a joke about the death of Lucas's partner Kevin McGee who had killed himself in 2009.

Lucas, now 40, shot back: *'Shame on you. I'm not joking. I think you should delete that tweet. It really upset me.'*

He signed off: "*I appreciate all the support on here over the past couple of years but it's time to shut down my Twitter account.*"

He has since reappeared on Twitter.

TROLLING MALE CELEBRITIES

Conservative Australian journalist Andrew Bolt had to leave his home and relocate his family after receiving escalating threats.

Video-game designer James Desborough said he was viciously threatened for defending the use of physical violence as a plot device in computer games.

Movie blogger Alex Sandell received a torrent of hate mail, abusive phone calls (some in the middle of the night) and sometimes to his relatives, after writing unflattering reviews of the first two *Lord of the Rings* movies.

Football blogger Charles Johnson moved to a gated community because of the threats he received after splitting with the right and embracing liberal policies.

ARE WE AT PEAK TROLL?

Are we, as *Time* magazine asked in a 2016 article, losing the internet to the culture of hate? Or are we nearing Peak Troll?

Some internet pundits like Brad Templeton say troll behaviour will soon subside because technology is growing sophisticated enough to weed them out altogether and peak troll is closer than we imagine.

Other internet experts, however, believe trolls are here to stay because their abusive, provocative comments give them a sense of power, amusement, and control.

Trolling addresses a psychological urge, says Steve Jones, communications professor at the University of Illinois at Chicago:

"*There's a fundamental need for some people to irk others, to raise their ire, to annoy and to kind of toy with other people's emotions. The Internet provides a phenomenally good medium in which to do so.*"

David Ardia, director of Harvard's Citizen Media Law Project, believes trolls and their comments may be of benefit because they expose the dark, hidden side of our society, one that people would prefer to ignore and which, if rejected, can fester and become dangerous:

"[Trolls] are our neighbours. They're people who live in our communities. They probably wouldn't make those same statements in person. But those are (their) views."

"I'm just some dude on the Internet, and somebody will tell me probably once or twice a day to kill myself… if I look back to my late teens, early twenties when I was struggling with depression—if I had endured somebody telling me once or twice a day to kill myself, as happens now—it would have worked."
Anil Dash (writer and veteran Twitter user)

ONLINE SELF-DEFENCE

Trolls are more easily dealt with than cyberbullies and cyberstalkers because trolls don't care who they provoke as long as they provoke someone. If their target refuses to take the bait, they will move on and try to rile another individual or group, at least on that occasion.

The following strategies are useful against trolls:

- **Ignore**: most trolls want a response and will move on if they don't get it.
- **Get someone else to read the comments**: If we enlist a thick-skinned ally to wade through the comments and alert us to threats, we can take appropriate action.
- **Disable comments**: a good strategy for those who have no desire to read what anyone else thinks of them or their posts, tweets, or videos.
- **Block:** This can work with trolls because they're happy to move on and harass others if their current target fails to take the bait. As we'll see, though, it's useless when it comes to dealing with cyberbullies and cyberstalkers.
- **Don't read the comments:** Then again, why bother with them at all if we're not going to read them? Disable instead.
- **Mute**: One of the most effective troll-busting strategies. It's less blunt than blocking and so is less likely to antagonise because a muted troll can still see our posts and can comment on them as well.
- **Expose**: Animatou Sow tweeted that a teenage boy was *"talking nonsense about diversity/race"* to her. She discovered his identity and

informed his school and parents. In another instance, she rang the employer of a man who had made racist comments and said: "H*ello. Here's what your employee is doing while he's representing you in a public space.*"

- **Exasperate**: A hundred white supremacists once trolled writer Celeste Ng. She tried blocking them but it failed. She was well acquainted with racist and sexist trolling, but when the supremacists finally got to her she resolved to deal with them differently by donating $10 to the American Civil Liberties Union (ACLU) each time she was trolled. In some instances, her trolls were doubly punished when she tweeted to them: "*Based on your comment, profile pic & feed, I'll donate to both the ACLU & Planned Parenthood on your behalf.*" When the trolling finally subsided, Ng had donated about $200.

- **Kill with kindness**: At the Rio Olympics in 2016, several female gymnasts were bombarded with racist and body-shaming attacks. Alexa Moreno, 22 at the time, was one of them. One troll tweeted a picture of Peppa Pig, with a caption that read, "*Exclusive images of Alexa Moreno following her gymnastics routine.*" and another, "*Alexa Moreno has the body of two gymnasts, a diet before going to Rio could have been good.*" Alexa weighs 45kg, which is actually at the lower end of a healthy weight for her 1.4m height. Her supporters successfully countered the trolls by flooding her Twitter feed with kind and supportive comments.

- **Intervene socially:** As we learned in the last lesson, discussions that start with negative comments are far more likely to attract troll remarks until the entire thread turns toxic. We can engineer the opposite effect, however, with a few simple tweaks. For example, we can alter the trajectory of a discussion if we give priority to positive, constructive comments at the very beginning of a comment thread. This increases the perception of politeness and affects the tone of people's interactions.

- **Clarify guidelines**: Web forums could pin acceptable behaviour and language guidelines at the top of the discussion page because research shows this does have a positive effect on participants and makes them less likely to troll.

- **Build personal resilience**: Chris Tolles is the chief executive officer of popular discussion forum Topix.com, which moderates 120 million pages a month. He says, "*Don't take the bait. Don't feed the trolls.*" He goes on to say: "*You just have to build defences against this kind of behaviour, because at the end of the day, all of their power comes from your reaction.*"

- **Listen to what the ex-trolls say**: Who better to advise on online self-defence than ex-trolls themselves. After all, they know a troll's motives better than anybody else. This advice from former troll Paul Jun is an excellent place to start.

THE INTERNET'S NEWEST ANTI-TROLL WEAPON

Until recently, moderators of social media, news sites, and forums have had few options when it comes to keeping discussions civilised. They can turn comments off completely, manually moderate them or assign upvote or downvote opportunities to users. But there's another option now.

In 2016, Jigsaw--a Google splinter group-- launched a project to foil online aggression with machines that learn. In February 2017, it introduced a piece of code called Perspective which uses machine learning to detect offensive speech, incivility, and harassment online.

When a sentence is typed into its interface, Perspective quickly assesses the phrase's "toxicity" with more accuracy and speed than a human moderator or a keyboard blacklist.

On its demonstration website, we can enter a phrase into Perspective's interface to instantaneously see how it rates on the "toxicity" scale.

Writing Experiment

What if you could see the potential impact of your trolling? Go here and see for yourself:

http://www.perspectiveapi.com/#/

CONCLUSION

Trolls are everywhere on the internet and their behaviour ranges from funny to annoying to hateful. Although they appear to want attention focused on their victim, trolls actually want the spotlight on themselves. If their target fails to take the bait, they will move on and harass someone else.

Surprisingly, many trolls do not fit the troll stereotype and given the right circumstances, any one of us can troll. While it's true that trolls can be extremely nasty and cruel, they generally confine themselves to online comments and rarely let their behaviour spill over into the physical world.

If their behaviour escalates to doxing or swatting or inciting their target to self-harm, however, they are then classified as cyberbullies or cyberstalkers and require a different response.

Trolls can be countered with a variety of strategies that range from muting to social interventions and machine learning.

Says comedian Ricky Gervais, no stranger to trolls himself:

"Never get upset by trolls. Expose them, Ignore them, Block them, whatever, but always know they "Never get upset by trolls. Expose them, Ignore them, Block them, whatever, but always know they are nowhere near as good as you. Smile."

Fortunately, these strategies usually work with trolls.

Unfortunately, they rarely work with cyberbullies and cyberstalkers and we'll see why in the following chapters.

CYBERSHAMING

In this chapter we will be looking at the phenomenon of cybershaming and how it differs from trolling. Specifically, we will:

- Identify the main characteristics of cybershaming
- Outline the ways in which people are cybershamed
- Describe the motivations behind cybershaming
- How to avoid being cybershamed

These days, online lynch mobs are free to shame anyone with a social media account.

This modern incarnation of an age-old practice is now so common that journalist Jon Ronson, author of *So You've Been Publically Shamed*, calls it "a social menace" with the power to ruin lives and reputations.

At the forefront of online shaming is social media, which Ronson describes as:

"A stage for constant artificial high drama [where] everyone is either a magnificent hero or a sickening villain."

But what exactly is it that drives us to shame a complete stranger online?

What motivates us to judge a person's entire character from one ill-advised, ironic, or politically incorrect tweet or Facebook post?

What impels us to pile on and dish out wildly disproportionate punishments, including rape and death threats, to people we have never met and of whom we know nothing?

What underlies the virulent return of this disturbing ritual of public humiliation and moral righteousness?

Will we find a way to deal with online vigilante squads, or will people's fear of public shaming make for a bland wasteland of mundane tweets and politically correct Facebook posts?

Is it possible for self-righteousness to soften?

Is it possible for us to declare:

"I do not agree with what you have to say, but I'll defend to the death your right to say it."

Can we ever, as Voltaire implored, think for ourselves *"and allow others the privilege to do so, too?"*

A common feature of pre-modern society was its cruel ritual of social shaming.

PUBLIC SHAMING

FISHMONGERS AND BUTCHERS WHO DECEIVED THEIR CUSTOMERS WERE PUT IN STOCKS WITH THEIR ROTTING PRODUCE PLACED UNDER THEIR NOSES AND MADE TO ENDURE THE INSULTS OF PASSERS-BY AND LOCAL STALLHOLDERS.

In medieval England, for example, public shaming was a routine way to humiliate people.

An inn-keeper who sold wine that was "*putrid, corrupt, and altogether unsound for human use*" was tied to a stake and had the blameworthy bottle poured over his head and then smashed.

Public toilet cleaners—known as gongfarmers—who dumped raw sewerage in the open streets during the reign of Henry V111 had to stand in their own barrels of excrement with a hat on their heads announcing their crime.

And in 1552, a man and a woman guilty of small-scale pig smuggling were forced to ride through London with an animal carcass around their necks and a crown of pigs' toes on their heads.

In Germany, unmarried, pregnant women endured a public punishment called "hide and hair" where state-authorised torturers stripped their shirts off, whipped their naked backs with sticks and then cut off their hair.

PRE-MODERN PUBLIC SHAMING TOOLS

The Scold's Bridle

In a bid to keep women meek and submissive as per biblical exhortations, "scolds"—women who nagged, moaned, or dared admonish a man—were punished with the Scold's Bridle.

The device consisted of an iron cage which fitted over a woman's entire head, muzzling her with a rectangular plate that thrust into her mouth, stifling her tongue and lacerating it if she kept talking.

The pillory

Since at least the 1400s, this hinged wooden-plank with holes for the head and hands was a common public-shaming tool. Anyone found guilty of fraud, conjuring, blasphemy, perjury, slander, attempted sodomy, spreading false news, or even issuing false dinner invitations, was apt to be pilloried.

Pilloried individuals had to stand in the busiest streets at high noon to ensure maximum exposure. Bystanders threw whatever they had on hand—rotten eggs and vegetables, offal, glass shards, bricks, and even dead cats and dogs—at the hapless wretches, many of whom were also at risk of slow strangulation if a rotten floorboard collapsed.

The Cucking Stool
The Cucking Stool was a waterside see-saw with a dangling chair, built for harlots, loud mouths and chiding women. A woman was loaded on a chair, swivelled over the water and dunked repeatedly to the delight of a large, enthusiastic crowd. Some women caught pneumonia during winter and some even died if the crowd got over-excited and demanded extra submersions.

WHY DID PUBLIC SHAMING DECLINE?
University of Chicago Law Professor Dan M. Kahan believes public shaming declined with the decline of community.

In pre-modern shame societies, we saw the same people everywhere: at home, at school, at the market, and in church. We knew our neighbours and pretty much everything about them.

In this hot bed of intimacy and familiarity, a loss of face could literally destroy our reputations and livelihoods.

These days, however, our communities are relatively impersonal and most of us know nothing about each other.

Our reputations are no longer linked to our immediate neighborhoods, so public humiliation has less power to ruin us.
Until social media came along and made our world small again.

JAIL VERSUS PUBLIC SHAMING
US judge Paul Lenz gives people a choice: spend time in jail or stand on the street wearing a sandwich board that reads, "I was stupid" or "I'm a thief" or "I stole from the dead."

Over the years, he's dispensed about 20 similar sentences and only a small minority of people choose the sandwich board option. In other words, they prefer to be incarcerated than publically shamed.

The rest of us are no different and we'll do pretty much anything to avoid public approbation.

THE DIGITAL VILLAGE AND THE RETURN OF PUBLIC SHAMING
Ritual public shaming in our culture may have disappeared from the streets and town squares by about the middle of the 19th century, but it never vanished entirely. Instead, it retreated indoors, into the family arena, where it lay in wait for its next public appearance: the advent of social media in the 21st century.

Social media's created a virtual village where it's all too easy to destroy others.

In an instant, we judge total strangers on the basis of a single tweet or Facebook post.

And the speed and reach of social media make public humiliation more destructive than ever.

Those who have their lives upturned by online shaming are, in the words of Jon Ronson, "*mostly unemployed, fired for their transgressions, and they seemed broken somehow — deeply confused and traumatised.*"

WHAT IS CYBERSHAMING?
Cybershaming is the 21st century's version of public humiliation.

According to Wikipedia:

Online shaming is a form of Internet vigilantism in which targets are publicly humiliated using technology like social and new media. Proponents of shaming see it as a form of online participation that allows hacktivists and cyber-dissidents to right injustices. Critics see it as a tool that encourages online mobs to destroy the reputation and careers of people or organizations who made perceived slights.

Modern public shaming isn't as bad as the pillory is it?

No, it's worse.

According to Australian criminologist John Braithwaite, cybershaming's effects are even more devastating than its pre-modern equivalents. This is because it represents a sudden, harsh collapse of the defences we have built around the separate parts of our lives.

It exposes, says Braithwaite, "*the worst side of the offender's business or professional self…to people whom he normally presents his churchgoing self, his golf-playing self, his fatherly self.*"

CALL-OUT CULTURE
"*The corporations don't want blandness or complexity. They want spikes of outrage.*" Jon Ronson

Russell Blackford lectures in Philosophy at the University of Newcastle, Australia. He describes cybershaming's prevalence as the symptom of a "call-out culture" where decent people are brutally set-upon by online lynch mobs for the most minor of transgressions.

THE RETURN OF THE STASI
Journalist Jon Ronson thinks cybershaming is much more than the digital equivalent of the stocks and pillory. He likens it more to the Stasi, the official state security service of East Germany prior to the fall of the Berlin Wall.

We've created, he says, "*this surveillance society where we are always looking for clues to our neighbours' secret inner evil.*"

WHEN ARE PEOPLE CYBERSHAMED?
If the online lynch mob decides we are shameworthy, we will be shamed.

This might happen if we express an unpopular, unusual, or politically incorrect opinion.

Racist commenters are a common target for cybershamers.

For example, the website Jezebel logged a collection of racist tweets made by teenagers about Barack Obama. Jezebel published the students' names, called their schools and notified the principals about their tweets. They also published details of the students' hobbies and interests which would jeopardise their chances of getting into college if administrators googled their names. Most of the students deleted their Twitter accounts, but a Google search quickly brings up references to their racist tweets.

Yes, you're racist
The "*Yes, you're racist*" Twitter handle has grown enormously since its

inception in 2012 with over 59,000 followers. Users search for the words, "*I'm not racist but*" and then retweet. The individual who originally tweeted the remark is then set-upon by users who follow the "*Yes, you're racist*" account.

And then there's Justine Sacco.

The cautionary tale of Justine Sacco
In 2013, New York-based Justine Sacco was doing well. She had a job she loved with the digital media conglomerate IAC as their global head of communications and was looking forward to spending Christmas with her family in Cape Town.

On December 20, 2013, she boarded a flight at Heathrow airport bound for South Africa, took her seat, curled up, and went to sleep.

Shortly before boarding, she had tweeted her 170 Twitter followers:

"*Going to Africa. Hope I don't get AIDS. Just kidding. I'm white!*"

It was meant to be a joke.

"*I thought there was no way that anyone could possibly think it was literal. Unfortunately, I am not a character on South Park or a comedian, so I had no business commenting on the epidemic in such a politically incorrect manner on a public platform.*"

To say the joke fell flat is an understatement: it fell badly, disastrously flat. One of her followers retweeted it to journalist Sam Biddle, who described it as :

"*A natural post. Twitter disasters are the quickest source of outrage, and outrage is traffic. I didn't think about whether or not I would be ruining Sacco's life.*"

He immediately sent it to his thousands of followers.

Subsequently, Sacco's tweet unleashed "a 48-hour paroxysm of fury" that ended with her dismissal and her reputation trashed.

She slept for most of the journey and so had no clue about the growing rage on the ground.

A hashtag trended: #HasJustineLandedYet.

Outraged calls for her to be sacked led her employer to tweet:

"This is an outrageous, offensive comment. Employee in question currently unreachable on an int. flight."

Someone else tweeted:

*"We are about to watch this @JustineSacco b**ch get fired. In REAL time. Before she even KNOWS she's getting fired."*

When Sacco reached Cape Town several hours later, she was immediately sacked by IAC, received rape and death threats, and spent the next year hiding from public scorn.

"I cried my body weight out in the first 24 hours. You don't sleep. You wake up in the night forgetting where you are."

She made a public apology and left South Africa soon after, partly because hotel staff threatened to walk off the job if she stayed with them. Her family was angry and told her she'd damaged their reputation.

She had to leave New York and eventually found another job with a small start-up company, but the humiliation followed. She had trouble finding a date.

Buzzfeed even scoured her Twitter account to find further transgressions and published an article called Sixteen Tweets Justine Sacco Regrets.

AFTERMATH
"The internet is a mountain, and if you climb that mountain, waiting for you at the top will be the person with whom you need to make peace. I climbed my mountain and a woman named Justine Sacco was there."
~ Sam Biddle

Six months after Justine's horror story began on that fateful day, she emailed Sam Biddle, the journalist who retweeted her original message, and asked him if he'd like to meet her for dinner.

Biddle was nervous and half-way through dinner told her he was sorry for what he had done.

He has since made a public apology.

He saw for the first time that she is a human being and not a collection of pixels:

"And, as it turned out, Justine Sacco is not a racist monster. She is a kind and canny woman who threw back cocktails, ate delicately, and spoke expertly about software. She was friendly, very funny, instantly relatable, and very plainly not a cruel sicko. We talked about college, jobs, home, family, and work—she'd recently landed on her feet as the communications boss for a small New York start-up, and seemed to be happily rebuilding her career, was gracious and kind and did not in any way deserve the internet hate fest her ill-judged tweet unleashed."

A year later when Biddle himself was cybershamed, Sacco messaged him with this advice:

"Just don't engage."

Said Biddle:

"Without any discussion, she knew the only divine truth of the internet: Do nothing. Never tweet. Never apologize. Never say anything at all. Be an inert bundle of molecules and let the world tear itself apart around you."

PARENTS WHO CYBERSHAME

Parents are now taking to social media to shame their children, often with tragic consequences.

One father caught his 13-year-old daughter posing as a 19-year-old online and then forced her to face a camera and admit she still watches the Disney Channel.

Another father discovered his daughter had posted a twerking (mildly provocative dancing) video on Facebook. He then posted his own video showing him whipping her with a cable while she curled up and screamed in agony.

Another father had his son twirl for the camera in his favourite skinny jeans while saying *"it look like you stole a midget's pants"*. He then set it to music and posted it on YouTube.

Isabel Laxamana

13-year-old Izabel Laxamana took a picture of herself in a sport bra and leggings and sent it to a boy at her school. The school administration heard about the picture and told her parents, who had forbidden her to go on social media or to take selfies. They said they would cut off her hair if she did.

Her father went through with the threat, cut her hair to shoulder length and filmed it all.

The video soon appeared on YouTube.

Although people originally thought her father had posted the video on YouTube, the police subsequently found that Izabel herself had done so.

Consumed by shame, she then wrote a series of notes, left them with a friend and the next day jumped off an overpass into oncoming traffic. She died the following day.

The original YouTube video has since been viewed millions of times.

WHY ALL THE HATE?

A 2013 study from Beihang University in Beijing of Twitter-like site Weibo, found that anger spreads far more easily over social media than joy. Anger, it seems, is hugely rewarded on social media with Facebook "likes" and "shares" and endless Twitter re-tweets.

Psychology professor Ryan Martin, an anger specialist, says this is because we tend to mainly share happiness with our friends and family.

Outrage, on the other hand, is something we happily do with strangers because it gives us plenty of social validation. People want to feel vindicated and less lonely and isolated, says Martin, and they want to know that others feel like they do.

VIRTUE SIGNALLING

Virtue Signalling, aka, self-righteousnes, is a prominent feature of many online pile-ons.

It describes behaviour that is used to draw attention to one's moral fortitude.

Individuals who want to raise their standing in a group will express the purity of their personal views to show how virtuous they are. People who virtue signal will join a digital pile-on as a way to prop up their ego and to indicate moral superiority.

From the Urban Dictionary:

"Saying you love or hate something to show off what a virtuous person you are, instead of actually trying to fix the problem."

IMPULSIVITY AND RASHNESS

An even greater problem than virtue signalling, however, is our rashness.

Professor Ryan Martin says it's this rashness, coupled with outrage and its relationshiop to our easily accessible devices, that is the catalyst for online mobbing.

Says Martin:

"The Internet exacerbates impulse-control problems. You get mad, and you can tell the world about it in moments before you've had a chance to calm down and think things through."

THE SHADOW

Swiss psychiatrist C.G.Jung coined this term for our metaphorical "dark side".

The shadow is the mysterious, shadier side of our personality that comprises primitive, negative impulses such as lust, selfishness, greed, envy, rage, and the hunger for power and control.

Whatever we deem evil, inferior, or unacceptable in ourselves becomes part of the shadow.

It's the opposite of our conscious, ego personality and we have no idea it's there.

This leaves us open to condemning the darkness in others without examining the darkness in ourselves. This is also known as projection. Jungian analyst Aniela Jaffe, describes the shadow as:

"The sum of all personal and collective psychic elements which, because of their incompatibility with the chosen conscious attitude, are denied expression in life."

Conclusion

"We need to think about when public criticism is fair and fitting, when it becomes disproportionate, and when it spirals down into something mean and brutal." ~ Professor Russell Blackford

Public humiliation is back in a much more virulent and devastating form than ever before.

In the blink of an eye, online vigilante squads can tear people apart and then move on to the next digital stoning.

Whether it's due to our individual and collective shadow, our rashness, or our need to appear morally upstanding, it's on the rise and ruining people's lives and mental health.

The punishment in many cases is way disproportionate to the scale of the perceived transgression and yet the irony of this seems to be lost on those who pile on mercilessly.

And, of course, vigilantism of all kinds involves the inability to acknowledge we are dealing with real human beings with real feelings.

CYBERBULLYING

In this chapter, we'll explore the psychology and tactics of cyberbullies, examine several cyberbullying case studies and note the strategies, innovative and conventional, put forward to combat it at a government, corporate, and individual level.

We will:

- Identify the main characteristics of cyberbullying
- Distinguish cyberbullying from other types of online harassment
- Describe the motivations behind cyberbullying
- Outline several practical responses to cyberbullying

A short history of the word bully

The word 'Bully' once had positive connotations.

ORIGINS — The word bully is thought to have been borrowed from Middle Dutch 'boele', which means lover.

1538 — First known English print appearance, bully refers to someone's 'sweetheart'.

1693 — Some negative associations emerge in print but still more commonly used to describe a 'fine chap,' or a boastful devil.

MID 1880S — Bully means 'excellent' thus replacing original meaning of sweetheart.

NOW — To treat (someone) in a cruel, insulting, threatening or aggressive fashion: to act like a bully toward".

"A blustering, browbeating person; especially one who is habitually cruel, insulting, or threatening to others who are weaker, smaller, or in some way vulnerable."

Source: Merriam-Webster Online

Cyberbullying refers to online abuse among teenagers and children, although adults who harass children are also considered cyberbullies.

Cyberbullying, unlike traditional bullying which is generally confined to school hours, continues 24/7/365.

This around-the-clock abuse allows its victims no safe refuge and often has devastating implications for their mental and physical health.

As technology advances, cyberbullies use it to harass their targets in increasingly sophisticated and varied ways and for new collaborators to join the fray all the time.

The situation looks intractable, but there is hope.

First, though, we need to understand what cyberbullying is, who the cyberbullies are, and what motivates them to drive some of their victims to suicide.

WHAT IS BULLYING?

Bullying is not occasional teasing, being pushed once, arguing with others, or having one's feelings accidentally hurt.

Rather, the Cyberbullying Research Centre (CRC) in the US defines it as follows:

"Bullying is harmful behaviour that continues over time and consists of intentional, repeated hurtful actions where the victim is unable to adequately defend themselves."

WHAT IS CYBERBULLYING?

As we learned in the chapter on trolls, cyberbullying resembles cyberstalking in every way but one: the victim's age.

Cyberbullying, says the CRC, is more aptly reserved for the kinds of behaviours that occur among adolescents, although it is also called cyberbullying if an adult harasses a child or teenager online.

When cyberbullying occurs in an adult context, it is referred to as cyberharassment or cyberstalking.

The CRC acknowledges that there is some debate about this distinction, but for reasons of clarity and simplicity, this is the definition we will also use in this lesson.

The CRC defines cyberbullying as:

"Wilful and repeated harm inflicted through the use of computers, cell phones, and other electronic devices."

This definition, they add, covers cyberbullying's most important elements, which are:

- **Wilfulness:** The behaviour is intentional and non-accidental
- **Repetition:** The bullying constitutes a behaviour pattern and is not an isolated incident
- **Harmfulness:** The target feels they were harmed by the bullying
- **Computers, cell phones, and other electronic devices** are used

The Bully Zero Australia Foundation defines cyberbullying as the use of :

"[T]he deliberate use of social media platforms, information and communication technologies, new media technologies i.e. (email, phones, The "Chatrooms, discussion groups, applications, instant messaging, blogs, video clips, cameras, hate websites/pages, blogs and gaming sites) to repeatedly harass, threaten, humiliate and victimise another with the intention to cause harm, reputation damage, discomfort and intimidation."

According to the Office of the eSafety Commissioner in Australia, cyberbullying is:

"[T]he use of technology to bully a person or group with the intent to hurt them socially, psychologically or even physically."

CYBERBULLYNG VERSUS TRADITIONAL BULLYING

Cyberbullying resembles traditional bullying in many ways, but the differences are as follows:

- **Familiarity:** in traditional bullying the victim and bully always know each other—they have a relationship, albeit a flawed one—and the victim usually has a sense of why they are being targeted.

Cyberbullying victims, however, may or may not know the identity of their bully, or why they are being targeted.

- **Ease and longevity of sharing:** In cyberbullying, the content used to humiliate a person can be spread and shared easily among many people and be accessible to anyone with internet access indefinitely. Traditional bullying, however, is localised, less able to be shared, and generally inaccessible to a wider audience.
- **Intensity:** Unlike traditional bullying which usually ends after school ends and the victim can retreat to the relative safety of their home, cyberbullying continues with 24/7/365 at school, work or home via social media, email, and mobile phones.
- **Power disparity:** All bullying involves some kind of power disparity. In traditional bullying, though, the power difference is far more obvious with the bully being more popular, physically stronger, or verbally intimidating than their victim. Cyberbullying's power imbalance is less obvious. For example, an online bully might simply have superior IT skills rather than be a member of the "cool" group or have a buffed physique. They might also have information, pictures or videos they can use to blackmail, embarrass and humiliate their victim.

CYBERBULLYING VS CYBERHARASSMENT

Research from the Cyberbullying Research Centre makes a distinction between harassment and bullying:

"Bullying is more repetitive than harassment (although, of course, harassment can be hurtful to the victim, it's just not bullying). Bullying is actually harassment taken to the next level."

WHO GETS CYBERBULLIED?

It could be any young person.

In 2012, French psychologist Violane Kubiszewski found that about two thirds of those involved in cyberbullying, whether aggressors or targets, had no involvement in traditional bullying offline.

The upshot of this is that children who are bullied online are not necessarily the same children who are being bullied in-person offline.

WHO ARE THE CYBERBULLIES?

The Cyberbullying Research Centre's Justin W. Patchin and Sameer

Hinduja surveyed two thousand students in thirty middle schools in Grades Six to Eight in Florida. Students who reported strain—financial, emotional, academic, and domestic—were "significantly" more likely to have bullied or cyberbullied others.

Similarly, Australian researcher Marilyn A. Campbell and her team at the Queensland University of Technology, found that cyberbullies have more social difficulties, are more stressed, anxious and depressed than non-cyberbullies and that they show no empathy for their targets.

It turns out that most bullies may not even consider their behaviour bullying.

Campbell's research also found that:

"Most students who are cyberbullies (aged 10-19) did not think that their bullying was harsh or that they had an impact on their victims."

Could it be that many individuals simply do not know how to behave in a civilised manner online?

WHAT MOTIVATES CYBERBULLIES?
Ongoing research attempts to isolate the motivations behind cyberbullying. At present, we have:

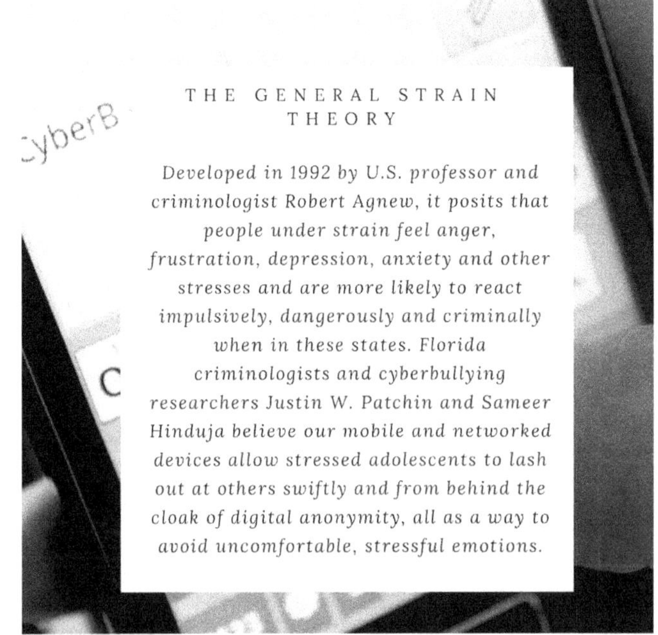

THE GENERAL STRAIN
THEORY

Developed in 1992 by U.S. professor and criminologist Robert Agnew, it posits that people under strain feel anger, frustration, depression, anxiety and other stresses and are more likely to react impulsively, dangerously and criminally when in these states. Florida criminologists and cyberbullying researchers Justin W. Patchin and Sameer Hinduja believe our mobile and networked devices allow stressed adolescents to lash out at others swiftly and from behind the cloak of digital anonymity, all as a way to avoid uncomfortable, stressful emotions.

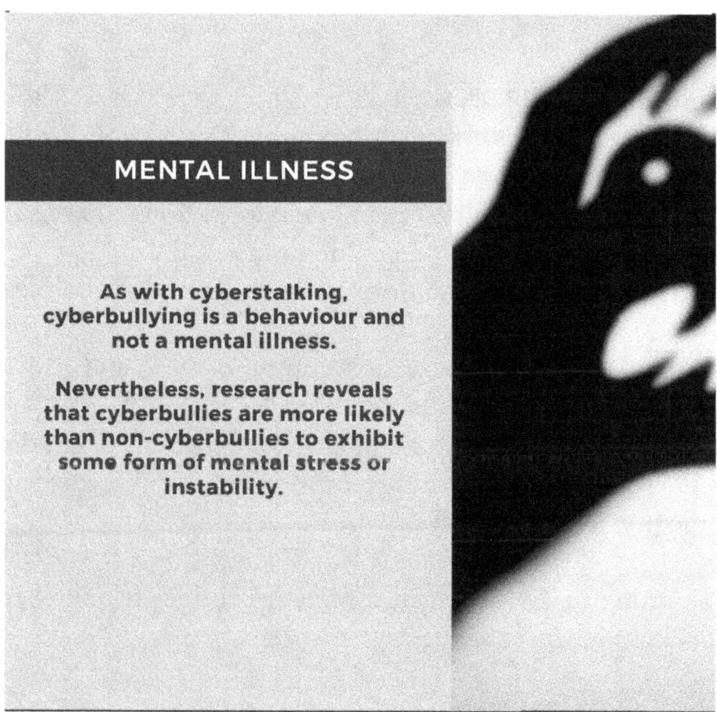

In 2012, Dr Frances Turcotte-Benedict and her colleagues at
Brown University, found that children with Oppositional Defiance
Disorder(ODD) were six times as likely to be perceived as bullies than
their non-ODD cohorts. Also, those with anxiety and Attention Deficit
Disorder and other mental disturbances were three times as likely to be
bullies.

This has serious implications given that studies conducted by the Centres
for Disease Control and Prevention in the U.S. estimate that between
13 and 20 percent of American children experience a mental disorder
in a given year. This represents a significant proportion of mentally
unstable adolescents who have the potential to cyberbully given the right
circumstances.

THE SITUATION IN AUSTRALIA

In 2015, the Australian Government released the results of their Child and
Adolescent Survey of Mental Health and Wellbeing.

The survey found:

- Almost one in seven (13.9%) of 4-17 year-olds were assessed as having a mental disorder in the previous 12 months. This is equivalent to 560,000 Australian children and adolescents.
- Males (16.3%) were more likely than females (11.5%) to have suffered from mental disorders in the preceding twelve months.
- ADHD was the most common disorder in children and adolescents (7.4%).
- Anxiety disorders were the next most common(6.9%) and
- 2.8% had a major depressive disorder.
- Almost one third (30.0%, or 4.2% of all 4-17 year-olds) of children and adolescents with a disorder had two or more mental disorders at some time in the previous 12 months.

Frontal Lobe immaturity: Teenagers' brains are physically unable to consider behavioural consequences.

Deborah Yurgelun-Todd and colleagues at the McLean Hospital Brain Imaging Center in Boston, Massachusetts, used functional magnetic resonance imaging to compare the activity of teenage brains to those of adults. They found that when adults process emotions, their frontal lobes are more active than a teenager's and that an adult's amygdala is less active than their teenage counterparts.

The frontal lobes are involved with emotional control and decisions about right and wrong and cause and effect.

The amygdala is part of the brain's limbic system and controls instinctive reactions such as the "fight, flight or freeze" responses.

Frontal lobe immaturity means children and teenagers have limited control over their behavior and emotions while an overactive amygdala is associated with high levels of emotional reactivity and impulsiveness.

The results from the McLean study suggest that while adults are more rational when it comes to emotional decisions, children and adolescents do not yet have the brain capacity to do the same.

When it comes to the volatile world of social media, this means children and teenagers text first and think later.

The Cigarette Effect: Coined by journalist Paula Todd who describes it as "the tendency to adopt rogue behaviour in the hopes of being perceived as "cool", it is today's equivalent of smoking behind the school sheds with the popular kids in a bid to look tough and cool themselves.

CHARACTERISTICS OF CYBERBULLYING

Cyberbullies may:
- send offensive or intimidating emails, texts, or voice mail
- threaten to humiliate, injure, or kill their target or their target's family or friends
- share—or threaten to share—photos, videos, personal information, or anything that may damage their target personally
- Photoshop images of the victim transposed over sexual imagery or other people's bodies
- make hoax calls to emergency services in the hope of sending armed officers to their target's home (swatting)
- forge intimate sexual invitations that appear to be from the target and send it to classmates and teachers
- create false Facebook accounts in their target's name
- commit physical or online attacks
- exclude their target online
- engage in nasty online gossip and chat\
- post vicious rumors
- follow their target around online, into chat rooms and favorite websites
- build fake profiles or websites and pose as their target
- plant statements to provoke third-party stalking and harassment
- sign their target up for porn sites, e-mailing lists, and junk e-mail
- steal their victim's passwords and hack into their online accounts
- share intimate information, whether it be sexual, special problems, secrets
- share contact information that includes sexual invitations such as:"for a good time call", or "I am interested in [fill in the blank] sex…".
- reporting their target for real or provoked terms of service violations ("notify wars" or "warning wars")
- encourage others to share their top ten "hit lists," or ugly lists, or slut lists online and include their target in that list
- post and encourage others to post nasty comments on their victim's blog
- send threats to others or attack others while posing as their target
- register their victim's name and set up a bash website or profile

- post rude, abusive, or provocative comments using their target's identity—for example, insulting racial minorities at a website devoted to that racial group
- send spam or malware to others while posing as their target
- break the rules of a web site or service while posing as their victim
- establish a "vote for" site (like "hot or not?") designed to embarrass or humiliate their target
- launch a denial of service attack on their victim's website or blog

HOW COMMON IS CYBERBULLYING?

In Australia, 1 in 5 students aged 8-15 say they have experienced cyberbullying according to research commissioned by the Abbott government in 2013. In that same year, 75% of all Australian schools reported incidents of cyberbullying.

In the U.S., the Cyberbullying Research Centre surveyed a nationally-representative sample of 5,700 middle and high school students between the ages of 12 and 17. Data were collected between July and October, 2016

When asked about specific types of cyberbullying experienced in the past 30 days prior to the survey:
- 22.5% experienced mean or hurtful comments
- 20.1% reported rumor-spreading
- Twenty-six percent of the sample reported being cyberbullied in one or more of the eleven specific types reported, two or more times over the course of the previous 30 days
- Approximately 34% of students aged 11-14 experience cyberbullying in their lifetimes
- Approximately 12% of the students admitted to cyberbullying others at some point in their lifetime.

Posting mean comments online was the most commonly reported type of cyberbullying during the previous 30 days (7.1%).

CYBERBULLYING AND GENDER

According to research from the Cyberbullying Research Centre, adolescent girls are significantly more likely to experience cyberbullying in their lifetimes (36.7% vs. 30.5%).

This gap narrows, however, when experiences over the previous 30 days were considered.

Say the researchers:
"Boys were significantly more likely to report cyberbullying others during their lifetime (12.7% vs. 10.2%) and in the most recent 30 days (7.7% vs. 4.4%)."

The type of cyberbullying tends to differ by gender; girls were more likely to say someone spread rumors about them online while boys were more likely to say that someone threatened to hurt them online.

This was the first sample we have collected where boys reported significantly more involvement in every type of cyberbullying offending behavior we asked about."

WHAT DOES CYBERBULLYING DO TO ITS VICTIMS?

The case of Amanda Todd

In the late afternoon of October 10th, 2012, while her mother was out shopping, a 15-year-old Canadian girl killed herself.

Her death made headlines around the world.

Several weeks before her suicide, Amanda Michelle Todd had recorded a devastating YouTube video where she told her story of bullying, extortion, depression, drug use, and her previous suicide attempts.

She shot the nine-minute video in her bedroom. To date, it's had over 12 million views.

She told her story with flash cards and to the sentimental strains of "Hear You Me."

Her nightmare began in 2010 when she was just 13 years old. She was chatting online with a man who told her she was stunningly beautiful. At his request, she flashed her breasts and he took pictures.

About a year later he asked her to "put on a show" for him. When she refused, he got progressively more hostile and predatory.

He found her classmates on Facebook and sent a photo of her breasts to them.

Todd grew increasingly anxious, agoraphobic, panicky and depressed and turned to drugs and alcohol. She engaged in ill-considered sexual encounters, which ended up causing her to be ostracised by her classmates and ridiculed online and offline.

She attempted suicide several times. In one case, she drank a bottle of bleach and nearly died.

Her mother and father are separated and in a bid to start afresh, she moved to her father's place, changed schools and hoped the abuse would end.

But her predator used the internet to track her down and posted her topless photo as his Facebook profile picture.

She began cutting herself and was bashed at her new school. The Facebook abuse was shocking and relentless. She was tagged in conversations and so knew her classmates were talking about her.

After her suicide, her family's nightmare continued.

Her mother, Carol, is attacked daily by online abusers:

"It's all your fault your daughter died. You are personally responsible for her death with your blatant negligence. Why the fuck didn't you take away your whore daughter's webcam. Answer: because you're relieved that she's dead, and that you no longer have to compete for your ex-hubby's romantic attention. Can you really blame him? Fatty? Go kill yourself."

Even now, years after her death, fake websites appear and blame Amanda and her mother for the bullying and blackmail Amanda endured:

"So she slept around, flashed her boobs, then people told her she's a slut and she killed herself? Seems legit."

The harassment continues despite Facebook and police involvement. Carol says it gets worse around Amanda's birthday, the anniversary of her suicide, and whenever she is involved in raising mental health awareness.

Cyberbullying and its effects on academic achievement
The Cyberbullying Research Centre's 2015 survey asked students to tell

them if they had stayed home from school at any time during the last
school year because they were being (1) bullied at school or (2) bullied
online.

The survey found that:

* 18.5% of the 25 million 12-17 year olds in the United States have
  skipped school at some point in the last year because of bullying at
  school
* approximately 2%, or over 500,000 students, said they stayed home
  "many times" due to bullying
* about 80% of the students said they had been bullied at school
* 61% said they were bullied online in a way that really affected their
  ability to learn and feel safe at school
* students who had been bullied or cyberbullied were significantly less
  likely to report that they felt safe at their school
* specifically, 76% of students who were bullied at school (and only
  57% of students who had been cyberbullied) said they felt safe at their
  school as a point of comparison, over 95% of students who had not
  been bullied or cyberbullied felt safe at their school.

The researchers concluded:

*"Taken as a whole, these findings demonstrate the toll that bullying (both at
school and online) can have on the academic success of students."*

Cyberbullying around the world

The following link describes parents' attitudes to cyberbullying in 24
countries, including whether or not their child has been cyberbullied.

http://www.puresight.com/Cyberbullying/cyber-bullying-statistics.html
Source: Ipsos poll for Reuters News, January 2012, via Puresight.com

Cyberbullying and the law in Australia

Commonwealth legislation governs online stalking and harassment
behaviour. The crimes legislation amendment (telecommunications
offences and other measures Act) – (No. 2) 2004 makes it a crime to use a
carriage service to menace, harass or cause offence. The alleged individual
could be found guilty under – 474.17 A (1) if:

(a) Person uses a carriage service;
(b) Does so in a way (whether by method of use or content of a communication, or both) that reasonable persons would regard as being, in all circumstances;

- Menacing, harassing or offending;
- Penalty: Imprisonment of up to – 3 years.

How does it feel to be cyberbullied?

Cyberbullying victims often feel trapped because they see no escape from their tormentors who are able to harass them 24/7/365.

They may also feel:
- **overwhelmed**: The stress of being targeted leads to feelings of despair and a sense that the entire world has it in for them, especially if the bullying involves a mass pile-on.
- **vulnerable and powerless**. When bullying continues day and night through mobile devices and computers, there is no safe place, no refuge from the abuse. To a victim, it seems as if the bullies are everywhere.
- **fearful:** Cyberbullies are often anonymous and this leads to increasing feelings of fear. Not having any idea who's responsible can lead to paranoia and hypervigilance.
- **exposed and humiliated:** Bullying feels permanent in cyberspace and with good reason: once something is posted it can be reposted and shared indefinitely with the whole world
- **dissatisfied with their image:** Cyberbullyies often attack their victims when they are most vulnerable. This only exacerbates any feelings of unworthiness. Victims may respond to these feelings by harming themselves in some way. For instance, cutting themselves or going on a crash diet if called fat, or changing their appearance in some way in the hope the cyberbullying will stop
- **anger and a desire for vengeance:** Sometimes victims of cyberbullying will get so angry about how they are being treated that they will plot revenge and consider retaliation
- **life apathy:** relentless cyberbullying may cause its victims to lose hope and to feel that life is not worth living. They may lose interest in things they once enjoyed and spend less time interacting with family and friends. Depression, moodiness and suicidal ideation may occur.
- **lonely and isolated**: Cyberbullying may lead to the victim being excluded and ostracised by their peers. This is particularly devastating

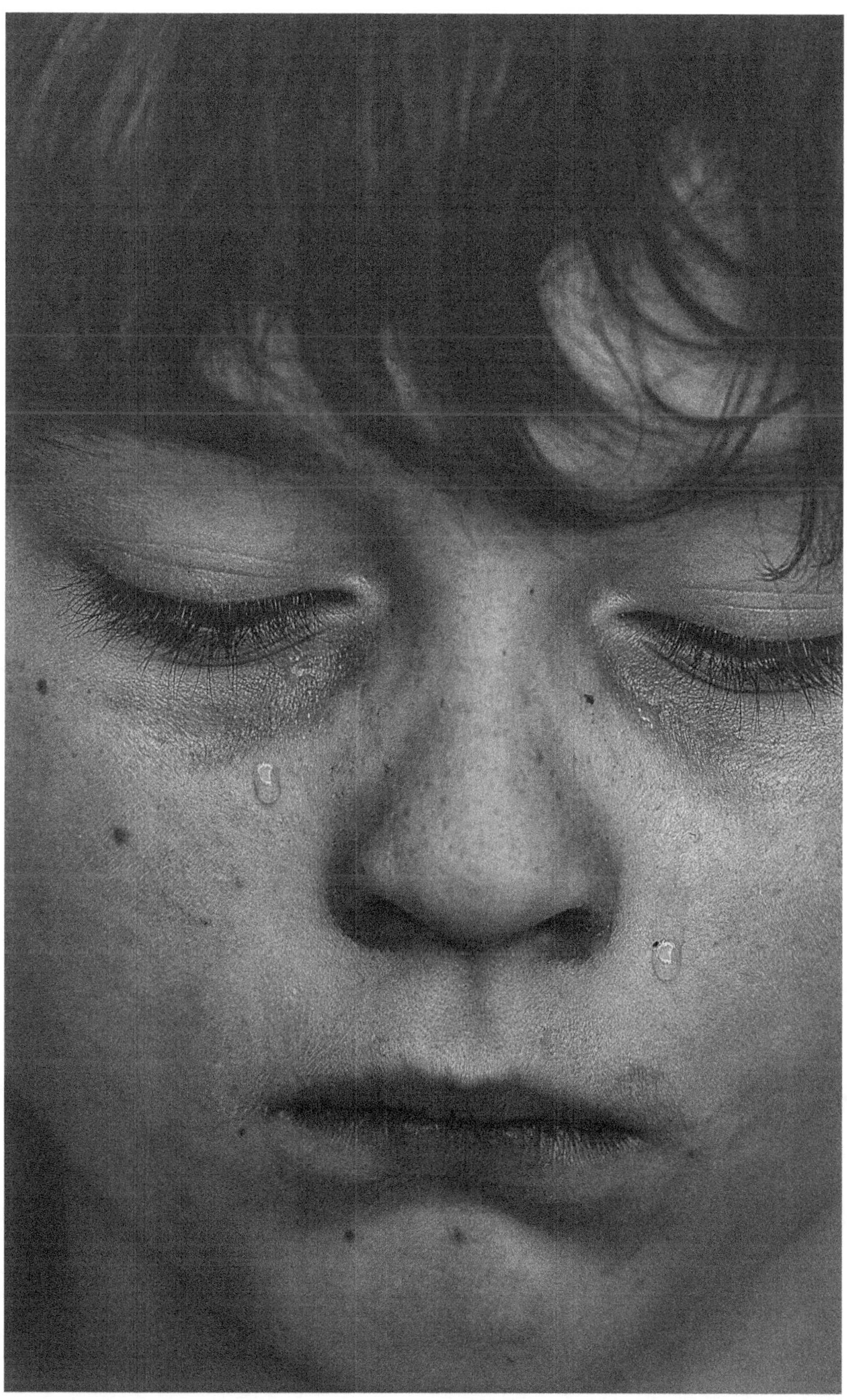

because when someone appears friendless, it can lead to worse bullying and increased feelings of worthlessness in the victim.

- **uninterested in school:** cyberbullying affects school attendance and academic achievement. Victims avoid school and do not want to face their peers because they are humiliated and embarrassed by the messages that were shared. Their marks suffer too because they find it difficult to concentrate or study because of the anxiety and stress the bullying causes.
- **anxious and depressed:** individuals who are cyberbullied are highly stressed and prone to develop anxiety, depression and other stress-related conditions.
- **unwell:** the stress of cyberbullying can lead to physical symptoms such as headaches, stomach upsets and other ailments such as stomach ulcers, insomnia, nightmares and skin conditions
- **suicidal.** Victims of cyberbullying are at an increased risk of suicide because the relentless harassment leads to feelings of hopelessness. Victims might feel so trapped by the harassment that the only way out they can see is suicide.

STRATEGIES TO PREVENT OR STOP CYBERBULLYING

1. The Australian eSafety Commissioner advises victims of cyberbullying to:
- Immediately talk to someone they can trust straight away
- Not retaliate or respond
- block the bully and change all their privacy settings
- report the abuse to the service and get others to as well
- collect the evidence—keep mobile phone messages, take screen shots and print emails or social networking conversations
- do something they enjoy—catch-up with friends, listen to good music, watch a good show or chat online to trustworthy people
- events.
- Develop a positive view about yourself and be confident in your strengths and abilities.
- Try to take a longer-term perspective and don't blow the significance of the event out of proportion.
- Stay hopeful and optimistic: Visualise what you want, rather than worrying about what you fear.
- Look after yourself – eat well, exercise, get plenty of sleep.

2. School talks

At 7:30am on Easter Saturday 2014, 18-year-old Jessica Cleyland texted her parents to say she was going for a run on a large rural property adjacent to theirs.

When she failed to reappear a few hours later and did not answer her mobile phone, her parents, Michael and Jane, went looking for her.

Said Michael:
We walked around for three hours and hadn't found her so I went back to the house. She still wasn't there so I started driving around in the car looking for her. I drove up the top of the hill and as I drove by something caught the corner of my eye and I found her."

Jessica had committed suicide.

"There were absolutely no signs that there was anything wrong. The whole family was devastated; we were all in shock.

The day after I found Jess, my eldest daughter Amy and myself started wondering what the hell had gone wrong. We still had her laptop and her iPad so we started looking through them and saw she had been cyber bullied the night before she died.

Two people were telling her that she was a sook, that she should just get over things, that 'if you come around to my place, I'm going to slam the door in your face. You're useless'.

There were 87 messages between the two and you could tell how hurt Jess was in the messages.

She was pleading with them just to stop but they relentlessly just kept going.

Jessica was 18, she was extremely popular in school, she was loving and caring.

Leading right up to Jessica's death there were no signs of depression, but she committed suicide after being cyber bullied."

Michael Cleyland told this story to a group of students at Glenroy College in Melbourne's north in 2015.

He's now an ambassador for the anti-bullying charity Bully Zero Australia Foundation established in 2013.

Bully Zero considers people like Michael to be an especially potent tool in their efforts to eradicate cyberbullying.

The organisation's chief executive, Oscar Yildiz says:

To have ambassadors who have actually been through a child's death after cyber bullying — they've been through that pain, they live the nightmare every day — to be able to express that to an audience of young teenagers is probably the most effective way of delivering these messages."

Student responses to Cleyland's talk appear to reinforce Yildiz's belief:

"He can't bring his daughter back, nothing can bring her back," student. *People need to stop and realise that bullying is serious and it's taking people's lives because of other people's immature and childish actions."*

"It does make me think more on what I say online and how I say it and what it means to other people and what it does to them mentally." Christian C.

"I thought it was interesting how we got an experience from somebody whose daughter has actually killed herself, because I've never actually talked to someone who's been through that. You see it on TV and in films, but you don't actually get the real deal." Matthew A.

3.Creative individual action

Positive Post-It Day began in the autumn of 2014 when Caitlin Haacke, a Canadian teenager, wanted to undermine the bullies.

She'd been bullied at school and harassed on Facebook with people telling her to kill herself. She decided to fight back by turning her feelings of anger into something more positive instead. She bought post-it notes and colourful markers and posted hundreds of hand-written notes around her school. Each note contained a simple, positive and compassionate message designed to uplift and bolster people's spirits. School administrators disciplined her at first for littering, but other students and parents supported her and she was allowed to continue her campaign. It is now a world-wide phenomenon.

4. Alerts

In 2014, 13-year-old Trisha Prabhu from Illinois, created an app for the Google Science Fair—an online competition for teens between 13 and 18.

She designed an alert system that got teens to consider their actions before posting anything harmful online. Her idea for the app originated when she read that young people's brains are insufficiently developed to consider the results of their actions.

She figured that if they were forced to reconsider their posts, texts or tweets with a cyber alert mechanism, it could make a huge difference.

"I hypothesized that if adolescents (ages 12-18) were provided an alert mechanism that suggested them to re-think their decision if they expressed willingness to post a mean/hurtful message on social media, the number of mean/hurtful messages that adolescents will be willing to post would be lesser than adolescents that are not provided with such an alert mechanism."

And it works.

When study participants were presented with an alert that asked them to rethink their actions before posting something hurtful, there was a 93.43 percent reduction in the number of adolescents willing to post abusive messages.

Says Prabhu:

"I am looking forward to a future where we have conquered cyber-bullying!"

5. Build a personal survival strategy

In the 1970s-80s, Dr Salvatore R Maddi of the University of Chicago carried out a landmark study of Illinois Bell Telephone workers. Maddi wanted to know why some people stayed well even during the stress of a major downsizing programme. He found that the most resilient people held three key beliefs, known as the three C's:

- **Commitment:** they strive to be involved in events rather than feeling isolated.
- **Control:** they try to control outcomes, rather than lapse into passivity and powerlessness.
- **Challenge:** they view stressful changes (whether positive or negative) as new learning opportunities

The American Psychological Association has studied resilience in-depth since the terrorist attacks of 9/11. They define resilience as the ability to adapt well in the face of adversity, trauma, tragedy, threats, and from sources of stress such as work pressures, health, family or relationship problems.

They offer these suggestions as a way to develop personal resilience:

- Develop supportive and caring relationships at home, among friends and colleagues. Accept help and support and help others when they need it.
- Remember that some crises are beyond your control. You can't change events but you can change the way you interpret and react to them. Try to accept this and look ahead.
- Accept that change is part of life and that you will have to adapt to changing circumstances.
- Set some realistic goals and take regular small steps towards achieving them. Ask yourself, "What's the one thing I can accomplish today?" rather than focusing on the overarching goal.
- Be decisive. Do as much as you can rather than avoiding problems and hoping they will go away.
- Try to understand your own experiences of dealing with loss, hardship or emotional problems. Appreciate what you have learned from these events.
- Develop a positive view about yourself and be confident in your strengths and abilities.
- Try to take a longer-term perspective and don't blow the significance of the event out of proportion.
- Stay hopeful and optimistic: Visualise what you want, rather than worrying about what you fear.
- Look after yourself – eat well, exercise, get plenty of sleep.

6. Major campaigns: Media, government, corporations
In 1975, the national Australian road toll stood at 3,634 and Australia's population was 13.89 million.

In 2015, the national Australian road toll had decreased to 1,209, a staggering decrease. This is phenomenal given that Australia's population nearly doubled in that time to nearly 25 million people.

What happened?

Newspaper campaigns

In 1969, 1034 people were killed on Victoria's roads. People thought the situation was hopeless. One newspaper—the Sun News Pictorial—ran a campaign called "Declare War on 1034", and although the road toll rose to 1061 the following year, it went down steadily in subsequent years. The campaign was so successful that it spawned drink-driving laws, random breath testing, and compulsory seatbelts.

The Transport Accident Commission (TAC)

On 10th December, 1989, the TAC, a Victorian no-fault accident compensation scheme, began an ad campaign designed to reduce the road toll in Victoria, Australia. It was a stunning success.

When the ad was first televised in 1989, the Victorian road toll was 776. By 2012, it had fallen to 303.
The ads were confronting and terrifying and had a huge and ongoing impact on the road toll statistics.

GOVERNMENT ACTION

In 1970, the Victorian state government became the first government in the western world to make seatbelt wearing compulsory. The remaining Australian states followed within 14 months and by 1977, 90% of drivers and passengers were buckling up. This led to a significant and lasting reduction in road deaths and injuries and became the single most effective method available for the protection of vehicle occupants in road crashes.

What's all this got to do with cyberbullying?

Strenuous government action by way of legislative change, corporate campaigns such as Declare War on 1034 and creative individual action such as Positive Post-It Day can eventually turn impossible situations around.

CONCLUSION

Cyberbullying will increase as more people go online and technology improves.

Unlike traditional bullying, which it victims can escape in the safety of their homes, cyberbullying continues 24/7/365 and it invades every nook and cranny of its victim's life with devastating consequences.

In this chapter, we explored the psychology and tactics of cyberbullies, and looked at several cyberbullying case studies and noted the strategies, innovative and conventional, put forward to combat it at a governmental, corporate and individual level.

The most promising solutions to cyberbullying come from Bully Zero's idea to have parents of cyberbullied children talk to students and apps that alert teenagers to reconsider the content of texts or posts before sending or publishing them.

In the end, though, we have to get serious. Reducing cyberbullying will require systemic social change. This will only happen with legislative review, better police training, internet civics education in all schools, and, most importantly, a government and business community prepared to commit to an anti-cyberbullying campaign similar in intensity to Australia's hugely successful effort to reduce its national road toll in the early seventies and beyond.

CYBERSTALKERS

In this chapter we will examine one of the web's most persistent predators: the cyberstalker.

Using case studies and recent research, we'll look at what cyberstalking is, who the cyberstalkers are, what they do, who they target, and how to protect ourselves from them.

We will examine:

- The basics of cyberstalker psychology and behaviour
- How to minimise your chances of being cyberstalked
- How to deal with a cyberstalker
- The effects of cyberstalking on its victims
- The most common cyberstalker tactics

As we learned in the chapter on trolls, cyberstalkers are far more dangerous and menacing than online trolls.

While cyberstalkers and trolls appear outwardly similar, they are different creatures with different psychological needs and motivations.

While it's true that trolls can also be nasty, cruel and destructive, their comments tend to be one-off and they will move on and provoke someone else if their target ignores the bait, at least on that occasion. As one troll said to journalist Paula Todd, author of *Extreme Mean*:

"Don't react to it. If I were to say that stuff and nobody responded, I am not going any further. I have nothing else to feed off. When you say something, I draw something from that just to continue."

When an individual or group is trolled for any length of time by the same person or gang, it becomes cyberbullying or cyberstalking instead.

Cyberstalkers fixate on a specific individual and will go to great lengths to get their attention. Their behaviour grows increasingly extreme and escalates to the point where it often spills over into the real, physical world.

Obsessive people like this are hard to dislodge and represent a formidable danger to the mental and physical health of their targets. So if we are to have any hope of stopping them, we must discover who they are and why they behave as they do.

STALKING DEFINED
A stalker is an individual who constantly trails, watches, or communicates with someone who makes it clear they do not want the attention.

Technology ethics professor Lambèr Royakkers says stalking, online or offline, is conducted by a person who has no current relationship with their victim.

He describes it as:

"[A form of] mental assault in which the perpetrator repeatedly, unwantedly, and disruptively breaks into the life-world of the victim, with whom he has no relationship (or no longer has), with motives that are directly or indirectly traceable to the affective sphere."

Cyberstalking

Cyberstalking, as defined in Australia by the Office of the eSafety Commissioner, is:

"[u]sing technology to stalk or repeatedly harass another person."

Although cyberstalking is a behaviour rather than a mental illness, studies in Australia and America indicate that a significant proportion of stalkers who end up in the courts suffer from some kind of mental disturbance. And the internet's vast, ever-shifting nature could be partly to blame.

In her book *Extreme Mean*, journalist Paula Todd describes a possible link between psychotic illness and social media. The internet, she says, *"offers the mentally ill a cornucopia of new interests and obsessions, along with the ability to research other people's personal lives and form delusional attachments."*

Cyberstalkers focus on a specific individual or group and will go to extreme lengths to get a response. They work alone or as members of organised online gangs.

Who are the cyberstalkers?

The majority of cyberstalkers are men.

Many cyberstalkers have jobs, partners, and families and are not the unemployed, disaffected loners the stalker stereotype suggests.

Lone stalkers include spurned lovers, ex-spouses, work colleagues, former friends or acquaintances, and total strangers. They are usually motivated by revenge, rage, envy, jealousy, or the need for their target's attention. They may also be in it for the money and will use personal information to blackmail their victim.

In contrast, stalker gangs are in it purely for the entertainment. Like lone stalkers, they may or may not know their target. Cyberstalkers use multiple methods of torment.

Tactics

They may:
- send offensive or intimidating emails, texts, or voice mail

- threaten to humiliate, injure, or even murder their target or their target's family and friends
- share—or threaten to share—photos, videos, personal information, or anything that may damage their target personally or professionally
- set up blogs or websites to undermine their victim as per Patrick Fox:
- make hoax calls to emergency services with the intention of luring armed officers to their target's address—this is known as "swatting" and it is turning deadly. See the case of William Moreno and the Andrew Finch case study below
- hack into or trawl through their target's email or social media accounts to find personal information or to reset passwords
- impersonate their target's online identity and send abusive messages to friends and family as a way to damage relationships
- empty bank accounts
- ruin their target's credit rating
- monitor their victim's movements using GPS, tracking apps, or spyware
- post false and malicious rumours on blogs or social media
- deface tribute sites set-up to honor dead teenagers and harass their family and friends via social media, email, phone, or text
- physically harm their victims in the real world
- enter or loiter outside or near the victim's residence, place of business, or any other place frequented by the person
- interfere with the victim's possessions or property, whether or not the person has an interest in the property, and
- physically assault their targets with an online attack.

WHEN SWATTING GOES HORRIBLY WRONG: THE TRAGIC CASE OF ANDREW FINCH

Wichita, Kansas, December 28, 2017, just before 6pm…

On a cold winter's evening just after Christmas, Andrew Finch opened the front door of his house to find it surrounded by armed police. Bewildered, he did what they told him and put his hands in the air.

His mother Lisa Finch, said she heard her son scream followed by the sound of gunfire. By the time she got to the door, her son lay dying on the porch, shot by an experienced police officer who thought he saw Finch reaching for a weapon.

Finch was unarmed.

Police then handcuffed his mother, her young granddaughter, and other household members and drove them in separate cars to the police station where they were interviewed. As they left the house, they all had to step over Finch's bleeding body. Said his mother, "*They didn't call the ambulance until he was dead.*"

How did this happen?

"*They call it swatting. I didn't even know it was a thing.*" ~ Lisa Finch

Andrew Finch was just 28 years old with two young children aged 2 and 7 when he became the innocent victim of a swatting attack where police had responded to what they believed was a murder and hostage situation.

No-one was dead and no-one was a hostage.

It was all a stupid hoax.

The deadly prank originated on Twitter after two *Call of Duty* video gamers got into an argument over a $2 bet. One of the gamers dared the other to swat him and tweeted a random address that was not his.

It was at this point that the aggrieved player likely enlisted the services of serial bomb hoaxer and swatter "Swautistic", who later told a reporter:

"I was minding my own business at the library and someone contacted me and said, 'Hey dude, this f—ing r—-d just gave me his address and he thinks nothing is going to happen. You want to prove him wrong?' I said, 'Sure, I love swatting kids who think that nothing's going to happen.' "
That evening, a man believed to be Swautistic ended up speaking with a 911 dispatcher. He told them he'd accidentally shot his father during an argument and now had a handgun pointed at hostages. He gave Finch's address and repeatedly asked the operator: "Do you have my address correct?"

The man kept calling 911 even after the police got to Finch's property.

The police quickly surrounded the two-storey house and Finch went to the front door. Seconds later, he lay mortally wounded on his porch.

Several days after he was shot, Los Angeles police arrested a man called Tyler R. Barriss and confirmed that was a suspect. The investigation is ongoing at the time of writing.

"I DIDN'T GET ANYONE KILLED BECAUSE I DIDN'T DISCHARGE A WEAPON AND BEING A SWAT MEMBER ISN'T MY PROFESSION," ~ Swautistic

US Epilepsy Foundation attack: when things get physical

In 2008, a stalker syndicate—attributed to a hardcore faction of the online hacktivist group Anonymous (although Anonymous strenuously denies this)—attacked the US Epilepsy Foundation's support message board.

Hackers created flashing animation at a frequency known to trigger seizures in photosensitive epileptics. Message board users clicked on what looked like innocuous-sounding titles and were exposed to these rapidly pulsating images.

IT worker RyAnne Fultz was one of those users. Fultz, 33 at the time, suffers from pattern-sensitive epilepsy and when she encountered the rapidly flashing colors, she could not look away. Fortunately, her 11-year-old son noticed something was up, distracted her gaze away from the computer and turned off the browser. But she was already having a seizure:

"I don't fall over and convulse, but it hurts... I was on the phone when it happened, and I couldn't move and couldn't speak. It was a spike of pain in my head…And the lockup, that only happens with really bad ones. I don't think I've had a seizure like that in about a year."

Browen Mead, another photosensitive epileptic, found herself with a day-long migraine after remaining too long on the site trying to find out who committed the attack.

Although this appears to be a one-off incident, it qualifies as cyberstalking rather than trolling due to its predatory nature and the seriousness of its effects. Its ramifications were felt in the real physical world and it's likely the hackers would have tried again if the Epilepsy Foundation's website had remained vulnerable to attack.

#Cut for Bieber attack

On January 4th, 2013, paparazzi snapped Justin Bieber smoking marijuana and the images were soon all over the internet. Bieber's teen fan base became inconsolable and a member of the notorious troll/stalker forum 4chan's /b/ board suggested Bieber's fans self-harm themselves as a way to persuade Bieber off drugs.

Fans complied and dozens of pictures, some of which may have been fake, appeared on Twitter depicting young fans bleeding from their cuts.

Cyberstalking and its effects

Cyberstalking causes severe emotional and physical distress. It can escalate quickly and develop into online and offline physical abuse. The longer it continues, the higher the chances its victims will be severely traumatised. People have lost their jobs, had nervous breakdowns, contemplated or attempted suicide, or become financially destitute after persistent cyberstalking.

Women and Cbyerstalking

Women are more likely to be cyberstalked than men. As we learnt in Rise of the Trolls, online abusers see women as easier to upset, which makes them ideal entertainment for stalker gangs.

Australian journalist Ginger Gorman interviewed and corresponded with a number of women who have been cyberstalked.

One woman emailed Gorman with:

"After we changed our mobile numbers, the harassment escalated and he began targeting my husband at his job and my kids' school. We have just decided to move out of state and I hope we can start fresh but deep down, I know he will find us…I just don't know how I can escape someone who is out to destroy me and my family."

The case of kathy sierra

In 2007, Kathy Sierra, a high-profile tech-specialist, game developer and programming instructor, wrote on her private blog: "I'm not moderating my blog comments, but I support those who do and here's why."

She believes some individuals took her remark as an attack on free speech and it triggered an avalanche of ferocious online and offline abuse that continued for weeks.

She received rape and death threats via email and blog posts, with one post featuring her picture next to a noose. Her social security number, home address and a mostly fabricated, highly detailed, and explicitly sordid account of her personal and employment history were all posted in open-letter-like fashion to *"pretty much everyone on the internet"*.

The document was also posted on her Wikipedia page.

Her family were threatened and people were encouraged to send things to her home.

She had, she said, *"every reason to believe this would continue to escalate if I didn't, well, stop 'serving the Koolaid'.*

Sierra subsequently left her job, rarely appeared anywhere in public and disappeared from the internet for the next six years, saying:

"I have cancelled all speaking engagements. I am afraid to leave my yard. I will never feel the same. I will never be the same."

Eventually, she returned to the internet but maintains a pessimistic view of what the law can do to protect us from cyberharassment:

"You're probably more likely to win the lottery than to get any law enforcement agency in the United States to take action when you are harassed online, no matter how viciously and explicitly. Local agencies lack the resources, federal agencies won't bother. (Unless you're a huge important celebrity. But the rules are always different for them. But trolls are quite happy to attack people who lack the resources to do anything about it. Troll code totally supports punching DOWN. There IS no "the authorities" that will help us. We are on our own. And if we don't take care of one another, nobody else will. We are all we've got."

RONI JACOBSON
Roni Jacobson had a stalker for 15 years. She first met Danny at a school camp when she was 12 and he was a few years older. They became friends and spoke with each other intermittently over the next school year. Eventually, however, he began to call her everyday. Johnson ignored his

calls, but when this had no effect, she blocked his number.

In 2006, Danny found her again on Facebook and unwilling to appear rude she accepted his friend request. He proceeded to send her long and digressive accounts of his day-to-day life to which she would respond occasionally.

His behaviour caused her little concern until her second year at college when she unexpectedly found him waiting for her outside the library. He gave her a CD and asked her to have dinner with him at the college café. She agreed because she wanted to be polite and, after an awkward dinner, left quickly.

She cut off all contact after this, but the Facebook messages increased to become daily updates on his life, political beliefs, job hunt, etc.

2012 was the last time she spoke with him and by this stage his messages had revved up to every few hours for three consecutive days. Jacobson asked him to "*please stop*" or she would have to block him.

To which Danny replied: "*Ok, good luck on your quest*" and proceeded to send her three more angry messages in a row. Jacobson blocked him.

"*His tactics update with every new technological advance.*"

Danny went "*nuts*" after this, she said, and called her names, threatened to destroy her career, and found new user names and ways to harass her when she blocked his texts or filtered his emails.

She submitted formal complaints to various authorities including the Federal Trade Commission, the New York State Attorney General, her local police, and the FBI, all to no avail.

The police were dismissive and told her that unless she felt scared and physically threatened, there was nothing they could do. This turned out to be untrue, but in the meantime Danny kept up the harassment and began to threaten her friends as well.

He ended up sending dozens of defamatory letters, emails, texts and Facebook messages to her family, friends, employers, professional organisations, and political offices. She found herself forever having to explain the situation to employers.

Over the years, Jacobson began to suspect that Danny had more than one victim, something she deduced from Danny's comments to her on social media.

One day, her father called to say Danny's lawyer had phoned him to apologise for Danny's behaviour and asked that Jacobson notify him if Danny ever attempted to contact her or anyone she knew ever again. This led Jacobson to suspect that one of Danny's other victim's was likely suing him, a tactic she feels will become increasingly common as people take cyberstalking into their own hands.

She believes her cyberstalking experience is drawing to a close with this latest development and hopes the law will find better and more efficient ways to deal with cyberstalkers.

As she says:

"I don' need the law questioning whether I feel scared enough. I just need my voice heard."

MEN AND CYBERSTALKING

The case of James Lasdun
In the autumn of 2003, British writer James Lasdun taught a creative writing class at a New York City college. His star student was an Iranian American woman in her early 30s who was writing a novel based on her family's experiences in Iran during the revolution.

Lasdun was immediately impressed with her clear and vigorous prose *"with [its] distinct fiery expressiveness in the more dramatic passages that made it a positive pleasure to read."*

In 2005, Nasreen (not her real name) contacted him to ask if he'd help edit her novel. Lasdun was busy but put her on to his literary agent who in turn directed her to a freelance editor. This appeared to please Nasreen and they corresponded amicably for some time until, he says, her emails became flirtatious.

Lasdun told her he was happily married and uninterested in an affair.

She seemed to take this well. They continued to correspond amicably for another few months until she began to send several emails a day. When he asked her to ease up a little, the emails became a deluge and their content took on a dark, disturbing, and vengeful tone.

Over the course of the next seven years, Nasreen continued to harass Lasdun relentlessly. She threatened to murder him and his family and found a way to impersonate his online identity so she could post comments and send emails purportedly from him.

She accused him of sleeping with his female students, of helping people to rape her, and of plagiarising her work and stealing the work of other writers

She told him she wanted to "ruin" him personally and professionally and wrote scathing reviews of his books and character on Amazon and in the comments section of his articles.

He had trouble sleeping and with trusting others. He found it hard to work and spent most of his days obsessing about Nasreen's motives and what she would do next. He began to have self-doubts and wondered what he might have done to provoke such hate and vitriol.

Law enforcement was of little help. A detective said that maybe they could call Nareen and ask her to stop.

Nasreen's abuse reached its nadir in August, 2012 with a series of twenty "extremely violent and threatening" messages on his answering machine. He digitally recorded them at the request of the New York Police Department's Hate Crimes Unit who considered the messages serious enough to have her extradited from California.

This never happened.

Nasreen had also been stalking other people, including Lasdun's literary agent and the freelance editor she'd been introduced to several years' prior. These two women were terrified of Nasreen being in New York and wandering the streets until her court appearance and asked Lasdun and the police to reconsider the extradition.

In 2013, Lasdun published his memoir *Give Me All You Have*, which is his riveting and harrowing account of the seven years he spent being cyberstalked.

In a 2014 interview, he said he hadn't heard from her since August 2012 when she left that terrifying barrage of messages on his voice mail. Despite this, he still thinks he's not seen the last of her.

COMMON REACTIONS TO CYBERSTALKING

People typically experience:

- confusion, anxiety, and a feeling of powerlessness
- anger and depression
- isolation from family and friends
- paranoia and a distrust of others
- insomnia
- nightmares
- hypervigilance
- thoughts of suicide
- disorganisation and a poor memory
- negative effects on their ability to work
- an inability to relax and unwind
- difficulty caring for others—children, parents, etc.

CYBERSTALKING AND THE LAW IN AUSTRALIA

Cyberstalking comes under the statutory provisions connected with offline stalking, which is illegal in all Australian states and territories.

Unfortunately, law enforcement is patchy and ineffective against all kinds of cyberharassment.

This piecemeal approach led Nigel Phair, Director of the Centre for Internet Safety at the University of Canberra, to say:

"Considering how much time individuals spend online, law enforcement capability – whether that be crime prevention investigation or anything in-between – is completely inadequate."

Even ACORN (the Australian Cybercrime Online Reporting Network) is, according to Phair, a *"bad user experience"* with *"no value to stop future victimisation."*

Ultimately, court action may be the only way to stop cyberstalking and this will need better police training, accurate stalking statistics, and legislative change.

OTHER OPTIONS

Cyberharassment expert Dr Emma Jane of the University of New South Wales, suggests more ways to combat cyberabuse, including cyberstalking. We need, she says:

- cyberethics education for schoolchildren
- ethics-driven software design
- social media companies to take more responsibility for the discourse that circulates on their platforms
- employers to step up and ensure the safety of staff who are required to be active on social media--this entails education about how to keep themselves safe online.

"The vast and destructive scourge of cyberhate and cyberviolence can not be erased by clicking your mouse. It's high time we stopped pretending otherwise and started looking for responses that adequately address the scale of the problem." Ginger Gorman, journalist

WHAT DO WE DO?

One day soon, the law and law enforcement will finally catch up with cyberstalking and move swiftly to counter it.

Until things improve and the web is no longer the Wild West, we must be as vigilant as possible with our personal information.

How to stay vigilant

1. Never post personal information on your social media accounts
It's way too tempting to share our lives on social media. We happily reveal our mobile phone numbers, home and email addresses, as well as pictures of our holidays, pets, family and friends. This makes it ridiculously easy for a stalker to find and manipulate us.

It's a devastating reality that members of organised cyberstalker gangs actively trawl the web to find vulnerable people and then use their personal information to harass them relentlessly.

So:
- Use a separate email account every time you register for social media apps
- Give each email account a bland, business-like name
- Never, ever post your home phone number, birthday, or real home address online, especially if you have public accounts.

2. Do a regular online name search
Even if we no longer provide our personal information online, family and friends might still be posting pictures of us. Cyberstalkers can use this information to construct devastating lies and fictitious documents as per Kathy Sierra who we met earlier.

To protect our personal details, we need to do a regular internet search of our name. If anything suspicious comes up, we can contact the website or the server administrator and request the content be removed.

3. Devise passwords that take 500 years to crack
Most of us have laughably easy passwords and online predators take advantage of our nonchalance, with disastrous consequences.

Cyberstalkers use a variety of methods to hack into their target's accounts and a weak password is a big security risk, so it's essential to devise a robust password.

So devise a strong password with at least eleven characters that is made up of upper and lower case letters, numbers and special characters like & or ^.

According to techradar.pro:

"To get an idea of the difference in security, let's assume a hacker gang with a fast computer can make 100 billion attempts per second to guess your password. Here's how long it might take:

- A short password made up of six random lower case letters - a fraction of a second
- A long password made up of 11 random lower case letters - 11 hours
- A long password made up of 11 random lower and upper case letters - two and a half years
- A long password made up of 11 random lower and upper case letters, numbers and special characters - 500 years."

4. Be wary of emails, texts, and phone calls that request personal information

Beware of anyone who claims to be a representative of a company who calls or emails with a survey which asks you to verify your identification and provide personal information. Decline, unless you are 100 percent sure of its provenance. Never, ever reveal your credit card identity pin or bank account details.

5. Change all account passwords when a relationship ends

A cyberstalker is often an abusive former partner. When leaving a relationship, change all passwords and create new online accounts. Banks must be told of this new relationship status and that the former partner is not permitted to access any new accounts.

6. Seek professional help

Alexis Moore is a US-based lawyer, cyberstalking expert and victim advocate who was stalked herself for years. She advises:

"If the harassment and stalking escalate and make you feel unsafe or threatened, it is important that you enlist the help of trained professionals. Aside from reporting the incident to law enforcement…seek the help of private investigators especially if the stalker's identity is still unknown. Reliable PIs conduct thorough surveillance and research to help find your online abuser and collect data against him. The faster you take action, the less chances the stalker can inflict permanent damage in your life."

7. Check out the anti-swatting and doxing task force Crash Override

Crash Override wants to help people avoid doxing and swatting and advises them on how to remove their personal information from online databases. It encourages people to develop a two-step verification process to make it harder for cyberstalkers to hack their social media accounts or emails and to keep them physically safe in the event this does happen.

8. Document every communication from a cyberstalker

Keep a record of every abusive tweet, email, voice message or real world sighting of a cyberstalker.

ALEXIS MOORE

Alexi Moore had recently left an abusive relationship when the stalking began. One day, as she swiped her credit card at the petrol browser a message appeared on the electronic board when she tried to lift the pump, "Please see the cashier." She tried another credit card. The same message appeared.

She wondered if her recent address change was responsible for the credit card problem.

Her ATM card didn't work either and stated there were insufficient funds. Alexis felt devastated when she realised all her money had vanished.

When she got home and did some investigation, she found that someone had closed all her credit cards, transferred money out of her bank account, and all the credit card companies and banks insisted that she had faxed them herself with the request.

Over the next few months, in addition to the cancelled credit cards and stolen money, her medical insurance was cut-off, her credit rating ruined and debt collectors appeared on her doorstep with false claims.

She deduced that the only person with enough information about her to do this was her abusive ex-partner. She knew she was in deep trouble because he had all her passwords, addresses, birthdate, and even her mother's maiden name. Moore calls him the absolute worst kind of stalker: "persistent, well-informed and malicious."

She became unable to work, lost all her money, and her credit rating was ruined. No one would give her an apartment, a car, a loan, or a job. She lost friends and family support. She eventually lost the will to live.

It was not until four years later that she recouped her finances became a writer, cybercrime expert and victim advocate.

It took Moore thousands of hours to repair her credit rating and to stop her cyberstalker's attacks, including having to make some difficult financial decisions. She also filed *"endless reports to the police, to the sheriff, the FBI and the district attorney's office"* as well as reaching out to people willing to help her.

Conclusion

Cyberstalking is the most serious form of internet harassment and its victims are left emotionally and physically traumatised.

Cyberstalkers are different from trolls and have different psychological needs. As such, they need to be treated differently.

Trolls will move on if ignored but cyberstalkers will become progressively more angry and threatening.

Cyberstalkers work alone or in gangs and are remarkably persistent. Their behaviour tends to escalate if blocked, muted, or ignored by their target. This makes them notoriously difficult to dislodge.

The law is piecemeal and inadequate when it comes to cyberstalking and this leads many victims to feel isolated and desperate. Nevertheless, pressure is building on government and law enforcement to take a tougher, more co-ordinated approach to hunting down and prosecuting cyberstalkers.

In the meantime, we must stay scrupulously vigilant about what we share online, document all communication from a cyberstalker and if we are stalked seek help immediately.

RESOURCES

TROLLS

WEBSITES AND BLOGS

Why do trolls troll? | *https://www.psychologytoday.com/blog/better-living-technology/201408/why-the- online-trolls- troll* | Viewed 23/8/2017

Why Blocking Trolls Doesn't Work |http://time.com/4457275/twitter-blocking-troll-failure/ | Viewed 31/8/2017

Online abusers ordinary people | http://www.dailymail.co.uk/news/article-4201908/Scientists-online-abusers-ordinary-people.html | Viewed 31/8/2017

Our experiments taught us why people troll | https://theconversation.com/our-experiments-taught-us-why-people-troll-72798 | Viewed 31/8/2017

Why are most trolls male? | http://www.telegraph.co.uk/men/thinking-man/why-are-most-internet-trolls-male/ | Viewed 1/9/2017

Stephen Fry Quits Twitter |http://www.telegraph.co.uk/news/2016/03/16/stephen-fry-quits-twitter-following-uproar-over-bag-lady-jibe/ | Viewed 1/9/2017

Internet trolling: quarter of teenagers suffered online abuse last year |https://www.theguardian.com/uk-news/2016/feb/09/internet-trolling-teenagers-online-abuse-hate-cyberbullying | Viewed 1/9/2017

Here's how many internet users there are | http://time.com/money/3896219/internet-users-worldwide/ | Viewed 4/9/2017

Mary Beard suffers "truly vile" online abuse on 'Question Time' |https://www.theguardian.com/media/2013/jan/21/mary-beard-suffers-twitter-abuse | https://www.theguardian.com/books/2013/jan/26/mary-beard-question-time-internet-trolls | Viewed 4/9/2017

Why trolls troll | https://theconversation.com/our-experiments-taught-us-why-people-troll-72798 | Viewed 4/9/2017

Why the trolls will always win |https://www.wired.com/2014/10/trolls-will-always-win/Viewed 4/9/2017

Interview with the trolls: we go after women because they are easier to hurt |http://www.news.com.au/technology/online/social/interviews-with-the-trolls-we-go-after-women-because-they-are-easier-to-hurt/news-story/c02bb2a5f8d7247d3fdd9aabe0f3ad26 | Viewed 4/9/2017

The first internet troll |https://www.gizmodo.com.au/2014/10/the-first-internet-troll/ | Viewed 4/9/2017

Trolls just want to have fun |http://www.sciencedirect.com/science/article/pii/S0191886914000324 | Viewed on 4/9/2017

Types of Internet Trolls |https://www.lifewire.com/types-of-internet-trolls-3485894 | Viewed on 4/9/2017

Trolling on Tinder and other dating apps: Examining the role of the Dark Tetrad and impulsivity |http://www.sciencedirect.com/science/article/pii/S0191886917300260?via%3Dihub | Viewed 4/9/2017

Exposed McCann troll was mired in loneliness |http://www.illawarramercury.com.au/story/2629697/exposed-mccann-troll-was-mired-in-loneliness/ | Viewed 4/9/2017

Who are trolls? |https://www.newstatesman.com/helen-lewis/2013/07/who-are-trolls | Viewed 6/9/2017

Twitter trolls jailed |https://www.independent.co.uk/news/uk/crime/twitter-trolls-isabella-sorley-and-john-nimmo-jailed-for-abusing-feminist-campaigner-caroline-criado-9083829.html | Viewed 8/9/2017

Bored Trolls | https://www.theguardian.com/commentisfree/2014/jan/09/malicious-tweets-caroline-criado-perez-boredom | Viewed 8/9/2017

Online disinhibition effect | https://www.learning-theories.com/online-disinhibition-effect-suler.html | Viewed 11/9/2017

Online harassment of women at risk of becoming established norm | https://www.theguardian.com/lifeandstyle/2016/mar/08/online-harassment-of-women-at-risk-of-becoming-established-norm-study | Viewed 12/9/2017

Higher proportion of men than women report online abuse in survey |

https://www.theguardian.com/media/2016/sep/06/higher-proportion-of-men-than-women-report-online-abuse-in-survey | Viewed 12/9/2017

Today's internet is a toxic wasteland | https://www.wired.com/2017/02/googles-troll-fighting-ai-now-belongs-world/ | Viewed 13/9/2017

What is turning so many young men into internet trolls? | https://www.theguardian.com/media/2013/aug/03/how-to-stop-trolls-social-media | Viewed 13/9/2017

Internet trolls are here to stay | http://articles.chicagotribune.com/2010-03-12/news/ct-met-trolls-on-the-internet-20100303_1_trolls-internet-anonymity | Viewed 12/9/2017

12 Things you never knew about 8Chan, the controversial message board | https://www.dailydot.com/unclick/8chan/ | Viewed 12/9/2017

Why we're losing the internet to the culture of hate | http://time.com/4457110/internet-trolls/ | Viewed 13/9/2017

Swedish model receives rape threats after posting image of hairylegs on Instagram | https://www.independent.co.uk/news/world/europe/instagram-model-hairy-legs-rape-threats-arvida-bystr-m-a7987496.html | Viewed 13/9/2017

The difference between a troll and a cyberbully | https://itstillworks.com/difference-between-troll-cyberbully-5054 | Viewed 18/9/2017

Trolling or Cyberbullying? Or Both? | https://www.psychologytoday.com/blog/teen-angst/201401/trolling-or-cyberbullying-or-both | Viewed 18/09/2017

Cyberhate: The block and mute buttons far from a key solution | http://thebigsmoke.com.au/2017/08/02/cyberhate-block-mute-buttons-far-key-solution/ | Viewed 18/9/2017

Ken M is the most epic troll on the internet | https://www.gizmodo.com.au/2015/10/ken-m-is-the-most-epic-troll-on-the-internet/ | Viewed 19/9/2017

Now anyone can deploy Google's troll fighting AI | https://www.wired.com/2017/02/googles-troll-fighting-ai-now-belongs-world/ | Viewed 20/9/2017

How I turned the tables on my trolls | http://www.dailymail.co.uk/news/article-2268558/How-I-turned-tables-trolls-Mary-Beard-suffered-vile-online-abuse-looks-appearing-Question-Time.html | Viewed 18/9/2017

Internet Troll Profile: 100 Internet Troll Profiles | https://www.ipredator.co/troll/

Absolutely everything you need to understand 4chan, the Internet's own bogeyman | https://www.washingtonpost.com/news/the-intersect/wp/2014/09/25/absolutely-everything-you-need-to-know-to-understand-4chan-the-internets-own-bogeyman/?utm_term=.ebe068763b01 | Viewed 21/9/2017

Internet trolls vote to send Taylor Swift to perform at school for the deaf | http://gawker.com/5939192/internet-trolls-vote-to-send-taylor-swift-to-perform-at-school-for-the-deaf | Viewed 22/9/2017

Don't let the trolls get you down | https://www.theguardian.com/education/2011/jun/13/internet-trolls-improbable-research | Viewed 22/9/2017

The cops don't care about violent online threats: what do we do now? | https://jezebel.com/the-cops-dont-care-about-violent-online-threats-what-d-1682577343 | Viewed 22/9/2017

Stephen Fry | http://www.stephenfry.com/2016/02/peedinthepool/ | Viewed 1/9/2017

Edge | https://www.edge.org/q2011/q11_4.html | Viewed 1/9/2017

Trolls | https://darkpsychology.co/troll/ | Viewed 4/9/2017

18 types of internet troll | http://www.smosh.com/smosh-pit/articles/18-%20types-of-%20internet-trolls | Viewed on 6/9/2017

BOOKS

Aiken, Mary, Dr: *The Cyber Effect,* John Murray (Publishers), UK, 2016, *Brewers Dictionary of Phrase and Fable*, Fifteenth Edition, Cassell Publishers Ltd, London, 1996

Todd, Paula, *Extreme Mean: Ending Cyberabuse at Work, School, and Home*, McClelland and Stewart, Random House, 2015

CYBERSTALKERS

I was a victim of cyberstalking |https://www.thoughtco.com/i-was-a-victim-of-cyberstalking-3534321 | Viewed 5/10/2017

Man creates revenge website to destroy ex-wife |https://jezebel.com/man-creates-revenge-website-to-destroy-ex-wife-says-he-1759871187 | Viewed 5/10/2017
The case of William Moreno |https://www.washingtonpost.com/local/crime/reign-of-terror-online-trolls-destroy-a-virginia-familys-offline-life/2015/07/20/a467f9bc-19ba-11e5-93b7-5eddc056ad8a_story.html?utm_term=.16625d87c4f9 | Viewed 6/10/2017

I've had a cyberstalker since I was 12 |https://www.wired.com/2016/02/ive-had-a-cyberstalker-since-i-was-12/ | Viewed 6/10/2017

Cyberstalking definition | https://en.wikipedia.org/wiki/Cyberstalking | Viewed 6/10/2017

Types of stalkers |https://www.stalkingriskprofile.com/what-is-stalking/types-of-stalking | Viewed 7/10/2017

Hackers assault epilepsy patients via computer |https://www.wired.com/2008/03/hackers-assault-epilepsy-patients-via-computer/ | Viewed 7/10/2017

How James Lusdan was haunted by a cyberstalker |http://www.telegraph.co.uk/culture/books/authorinterviews/9854693/How-James-Lasdun-was-haunted-by-a-cyberstalker.html | Viewed 8/10/2017

Cyberstalking and the law in Australia | http://www.findlaw.com.au/articles/4793/cyberstalking-and-the-law-.aspx | Viewed 10/10/2017

Cyberstalking: the fastest growing crime |https://www.psychologytoday.com/blog/sex-lies-trauma/201503/cyberstalking-the-fastest-growing-crime | Viewed 12/10/2017

Ten ways to make your passwords more secure | http://www.techradar.com/news/internet/policies-protocols/10-ways-to-make-your-passwords-secure-1155444 | Viewed 13/10/2017

They call it swatting https://arstechnica.com/tech-policy/2017/12/kansas-mans-death-may-have-resulted-from-call-of-duty-swatting/ Viewed 10/1/2018

Kansas man killed in swatting incident | https://www.rollingstone.com/glixel/news/newspaper-man-killed-in-call-of-duty-swatting-incident-w514820 Viewed 10/1/2018

Kansas man killed in SWATing attack | https://krebsonsecurity.com/2017/12/kansas-man-killed-in-swatting-attack/ Viewed 10/1/2018

Twitter user claims to have made the 'swatting' call that led police to kill a man | https://www.washingtonpost.com/news/post-nation/wp/2017/12/30/why-a-twitter-user-claims-to-have-made-the-swatting-call-that-led-police-to-kill-a-man/?utm_term=.6c3afabbabd0 Viewed 10/1/2018

CYBERSHAMING

WEBSITES AND BLOGS

Izabel Laxamana: a tragic case in the growing genre of parents publicly shaming their kids |http://www.slate.com/articles/technology/users/2015/06/izabel_laxamana_a_tragic_case_in_the_growing_genre_of_parents_publicly_shaming.html | Viewed 10/11/2017

The shame of public shaming |https://theconversation.com/the-shame-of-public-shaming-57584 | Viewed 10/11/2017

A ghoulish tour of medieval punishments |http://www.bbc.com/news/uk-england-36641921 | Viewed 10/11/2017

Jon Ronson on Monica Lewinsky and cybershaming | http://nymag.com/scienceofus/2015/03/jon-ronson-on-monica-lewinsky-and-cybershaming.html | Viewed 11/11/2017

Man chooses to hold "I was stupid" sign instead of jailtime | http://uk.legal.narkive.com/WUVlYJ6Z/man-chooses-to-hold-i-was-stupid-sign-instead-of-jail-time | Viewed 12/11/2017

Why you should think twice before shaming anyone on social media | https://www.wired.com/2013/07/ap_argshaming/ | Viewed 12/11/2017

How one stupid tweet blew up Justine Sacco's life |https://www.nytimes.com/2015/02/15/magazine/how-one-stupid-tweet-ruined-justine-saccos-life.html | Viewed 12/11/2017

Justine Sacco is good at her job and how I came to peace with her |http://gawker.com/justine-sacco-is-good-at-her-job-and-how-i-came-to-pea-1653022326 | Viewed 13/11/2017

Stasi | https://en.wikipedia.org/wiki/Stasi | Viewed 14/11/2017

Time and time again on Twitter, we act like the thing we purport to hate |https://www.theguardian.com/culture/2015/dec/13/jon-ronson-shame-bullying-twitter-social-media | Viewed 17/11/2017

Justine Sacco speaks about her experience one year after the tweet that ruined her life | http://www.news.com.au/technology/online/social/justine-sacco-speaks-about-her-experience-one-year-after-the-tweet-that-ruined-her-life/news-story/993b0788fdbda58794abb7ee53be04ed | Viewed 17/11/2017

Essential secrets of psychotherapy: what is the shadow? | https://www.psychologytoday.com/blog/evil-deeds/201204/essential-secrets-psychotherapy-what-is-the-shadow | Viewed 17/11/2017

List of motor vehicle deaths in Australia year by year | https://en.wikipedia.org/wiki/List_of_motor_vehicle_deaths_in_Australia_by_year | Viewed 17/11/2017

Why you should think twice before shaming anyone on social media | https://www.wired.com/2013/07/ap_argshaming/ | Viewed 17/11/2017

060ccef92686d9b0cda665fd74faba | Viewed 20/11/2017

WEBSITES AND BLOGS

Definition of cyberbullying | https://www.esafety.gov.au/esafety-information/esafety-issues/cyberbullying | Viewed 31/10/2017

Cyberbullying | https://en.wikipedia.org/wiki/Cyberbullying | Viewed 31/10/2017

2016 Cyberbullying Data | https://cyberbullying.org/2016-cyberbullying-data | Viewed 2/11/2017

Positive Post-it Day | https://cyberbullying.org/positive-post-it-day | Viewed 3/11/2017

1 in 5 Australian kids have experienced this. And the consequences can be devastating | https://www.mamamia.com.au/cyberbullying-statistics-in-australia/ | Viewed 3/11/2017

The case of Matthew Burdette | https://www.mamamia.com.au/matthew-burdette-suicide/ | Viewed 3/11/2017

Teen creates awesome science project that could help stop cyberbullying | http://www.huffingtonpost.com.au/entry/trisha-prabhu-google_n_5675110 | Viewed 3/11/2017

Stop Cyberbullying | http://www.stopcyberbullying.org/parents/telling_the_difference.html | Viewed 10/11/2017

Decision making is still a work in progress for teenagers | https://brainconnection.brainhq.com/2013/03/20/decision-making-is-still-a-work-in-progress-for-teenagers/ | 3/11/2017

Father crusades to stop cyberbullies after daughter's suicide | http://www.abc.net.au/news/2015-08-17/father-crusades-to-stop-cyber-bullies-after-daughters-suicide/6703668 | Viewed 6/11/2017

What are the effects of cyberbullying? | https://www.verywell.com/what-are-the-effects-of-cyberbullying-460558 | Viewed 6/11/2017
Resilience: how to build a personal strategy for survival | https://hbr.org/2009/01/resilience-how-to-build-a-pers | Viewed 7/11/2017

TAC 20 year anniversary retrospective montage "Everybody Hurts" | https://

www.tac.vic.gov.au/road-safety/tac-campaigns/20-year-campaign | Viewed 9/11/2017

The long road to a lower toll | http://www.theage.com.au/comment/the-age-editorial/the-long-road-to-a-lower-toll-20160101-glxt5x.html | Viewed 9/11/2017

Reduction in road fatalities and injuries after legislation for compulsory wearing of seat belts: experience in Victoria and the rest of Australia (Abstract) | https://www.ncbi.nlm.nih.gov/pubmed/466050 | Viewed 9/11/2017

Cyberbullying | https://www.esafety.gov.au/esafety-information/esafety-issues/cyberbullying | Viewed 9/11/2017

The definition of cyberbullying | https://cyberbullying.org/ | Viewed 9/11/2017

Responding to cyberbullying: top ten tips for teens | https://cyberbullying.org/responding-to-cyberbullying-top-ten-tips-for-teens | Viewed 9/11/2017

Cyberbullying is a crime | http://bzaf.org.au/cyber-bullying/ | Viewed 9/11/2017

www.ingramcontent.com/pod-product-compliance
Lightning Source LLC
Chambersburg PA
CBHW051002050726
47592CB00007B/2668